THE **TESTING** SERIES

NUMERICAL REASONING
TESTS

BY DAVID ISAACS

THE **TESTING** SERIES
expert advice on test preparation

 how2become

Orders: Please contact How2become Ltd, Suite 2, 50 Churchill Square Business Centre, Kings Hill, Kent ME19 4YU.

You can also order via the email address info@how2become.co.uk.

ISBN: 9781909229242

First published 2012

Typeset for How2become Ltd by Molly Hill, Canada.

Printed in Great Britain for How2become Ltd by CMP (uk) Limited, Poole, Dorset

NUMERICAL REASONING

Welcome to your guide to answering numerical reasoning questions. This book has been designed to increase your confidence and ability to answer mathematical questions which have every day meaning. For example, if you own a car the question might be how much does it cost to travel x amount of miles if the cost of fuel is y, or the question might ask you to calculate how much a designer jacket now costs after its original price is reduced by a certain percentage. Not only will these questions help you in everyday life calculations, but they will also help you succeed in your application for jobs which require you to have an ability to carry out numerical calculations.

A typical example of this might be an application to work in a job which involves handling money. As part of your application you will be asked to complete a numerical reasoning test.

This guide has been divided into two sections. The first section has 52 questions followed by 7 practice tests for you to try. During the first section I have deliberately provided the answers to each question immediately following each question. This will enable you to quickly check your answers, allowing you to improve and develop as you progress. For the final 7 practice tests the answers are provided after each test.

Good luck!

DAVID ISAACS

SECTION 1
52 QUESTIONS FOR YOU TO TRY

You do not have to complete them all at once, the key to improving is to take your time to understand why you went wrong if you did go wrong in the first place!

QUESTION 1

If you jog for 30 minutes and cover 5 miles, how many miles would you cover in 180 minutes, assuming your jogging speed remains constant?

    a) 60 miles

    b) 20 miles

    c) 30 miles

    d) 15 miles

ANSWER TO QUESTION 1

Use cross multiplication to solve this. Label the miles covered in 180 minutes as 'x':

30 minutes = 5 miles

180 minutes = x miles

$$30 \times x = 180 \times 5$$

Now find x:

$$x = (180 \times 5) \div 30$$

$$= 30 \text{ } miles$$

The answer to question 1 is **c)** 30 miles

QUESTION 2

A farm is split into 3 sections, A, B and C. If the area of all 3 sections combined is 250m² and the area of section A is 80m² work out the area of section B using the diagram below.

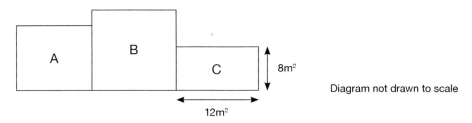

Diagram not drawn to scale

a) 32m²

b) 76m²

c) 74m²

d) 96m²

ANSWER TO QUESTION 2

The combined area of all 3 sections A, B and C is given as 250m² in the question and the area of section A only is given as 80m².

This means that the area of sections B and C combined must be:
250 – 80 = 170m²

It is possible to find the area of section C alone from the diagram and is calculated by multiplying the two sides together:

Area of section C is 12 × 8 = 96m²

The area of sections B and C combined is 170m² so the area of section B alone can be calculated by subtraction the area of C from the area of sections B and C combined as shown below:

Area of section B = *Area of sections B and C combined – Area of section C*

$$= 170 - 96$$

$$= 74m^2$$

The answer to question 2 is **c)** 74m²

QUESTION 3

A car can drive 650 miles on a full tank of diesel. If the car takes 60 litres of diesel to fill it's tank fully and each litre of diesel costs £1.35 how much would it cost to travel 650 miles?

a) £60

b) £61

c) £81

d) £95

ANSWER TO QUESTION 3

The car takes 60 litres of diesel to fill it's tank and once the tank is full the car can then travel 650 miles. Each litre of diesel cost's £1.35 so therefore the answer is that it costs 60 × £1.35 = £81 to fill the car up with diesel and with a full tank the car can then travel 650 miles. In other words it costs £81 to cover 650 miles by car.

The answer to question 3 is **c)** £81

QUESTION 4

A carpet factory operates 24 hours a day. If the factory produces 10 carpets an hour, how many carpets are produced in a day?

a) 220

b) 240

c) 260

d) 280

e) 290

ANSWER TO QUESTION 4

If the factory produces 10 carpets an hour then in 2 hours it produces 20 and in 3 hours produces 30 and in 4 hours produces 40 carpets and so on. The easiest way to calculate how many carpets are produced in a 24 hour period at the factory is to multiply 24 hours by 10 carpets because 10 carpets are produced every 1 hour:

Number of carpets produced in 24 hours: $24 \times 10 = 240$ carpets.

The answer to question 4 is b)

QUESTION 5

A builder needs 5 pieces of wood and has a plank of wood measuring 45 metres in length. If the builder chops the plank into 5 equal pieces what length would each of the 5 pieces be?

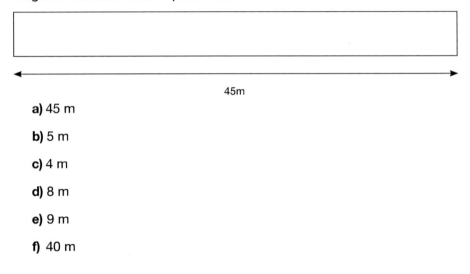

45m

a) 45 m

b) 5 m

c) 4 m

d) 8 m

e) 9 m

f) 40 m

ANSWER TO QUESTION 5

If a 45 m length plank is chopped into 5 equal pieces the calculation is $45 \div 5 = 9m$

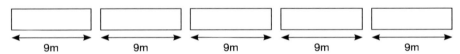

9m   9m   9m   9m   9m

Each piece is 9m long. The answer to question 5 is **e)** 9m

QUESTION 6

In a car park there are 120 cars. Five tenths of the cars in the car park are black. 3/5 of the black cars have five doors. How many black cars have five doors?

> **a)** 40
>
> **b)** 36
>
> **c)** 22
>
> **d)** 70
>
> **e)** 18

ANSWER TO QUESTION 6

In total there are 120 cars. Five tenths written as a fraction is 5/10 which is the same as 1/2 because both the top (numerator) and bottom (denominator) of the fraction can be divided by 5 in order to reduce the fraction 5/10 to its simplest form:

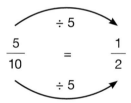

The question states that five tenths of the cars in the car park are black. In other words this means that half (1/2) of the 120 cars in the car park are black. To calculate the number of black cars in the car park, multiply 120 cars by either the decimal 0.5 or by the fraction 1/2. Both will give you the same answer because 0.5 is the decimal form of the fraction 1/2:

Number of black cars in the car park = 0.5 × 120

= 60

Or,

Number of black cars in the car park = 1/2 × 120

= 60

The question then states that 3/5 of the black cars have five doors. It is now known that there are 60 black cars in the car park. To find the amount of black cars with 5 doors simply multiply the total number of black cars in the car park (60) by 3/5.

Number of black cars with five doors $= 60 \times 3/5$

$= 36$ *cars*

The answer to question 6 is **b)** 36 black cars have five doors.

QUESTION 7

40 students sit an exam. 30 students get a grade A and the remainder get a grade B. What percentage of students got a B grade?

  a) 25%

  b) 50%

  c) 60%

  d) 47.5%

  e) 20.5%

ANSWER TO QUESTION 7

In total there are 40 students who sat the exam. 30 of these students passed with a grade A, therefore there are 40 – 30 = 10 students who got a grade B.

To write 10 students out of 40 as a percentage simply divide the two numbers and multiply by 100:

Percentage of students who got a grade B = $\dfrac{10}{40}$ × 100 = 25%

The answer to question 7 is **a)** 25% of the students got a grade B.

QUESTION 8

A train covers a distance of 10 miles in 30 minutes. What is the speed of the train in miles per hour?

    a) 10 mph

    b) 20 mph

    c) 30 mph

    d) 40 mph

    e) 45 mph

ANSWER TO QUESTION 8

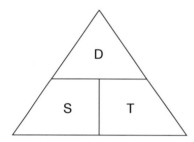

In the above triangle:

D represents Distance

S represents Speed

T represents Time.

If you wanted a formula to calculate speed, simply place your thumb over S on the triangle. You will now see that $S = D/T$

The formula to use here is:

$$Speed = \frac{distance\ (miles)}{time\ (hour)}$$

The distance covered by the train is 10 miles and the time it took was 30 minutes. However, be careful not to put 30 minutes directly into the formula when calculating the speed as you would get a wrong answer. The reason is that when you are using the speed equation shown above time is measured in 'hours' and not 'minutes'. This is because the question clearly states that it wants an answer in 'miles per hour' and not 'miles per minutes'. 30 minutes should therefore be converted into hours and how to do this is explained below.

Converting minutes into hours

To convert any amount of minutes into hours divide the minutes by 60.

30 minutes in hours = 30 ÷ 60 = 0.5 *hours*

30 minutes is half an hour. As a decimal this is 0.5 hours. Therefore 0.5 hours can be used in the speed formula to represent 30 minutes.

$$Speed = \frac{10\ (miles)}{0.5\ (hours)} = 20\ mph\ (miles\ per\ hour)$$

The answer to question 8 is **b)** 20 miles per hour

QUESTION 9

You are called to a meeting 120 miles away. It takes you 1 hour 30 minutes to arrive at the meeting site. What speed have you been driving at?

    a) 80

    b) 60

    c) 40

    d) 50

    e) 45

ANSWER TO QUESTION 9

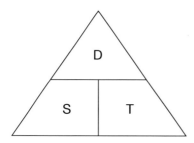

If you wanted a formula to calculate speed, simply place your thumb over S on the triangle. You will now see that $S = D/T$

The formula to use here is:

$$Speed = \frac{distance\ (miles)}{time\ (hour)}$$

The question gives the meeting distance as 120 miles away. Miles are the correct units to use for the formula and therefore 120 miles can be put straight into the formula without converting it to any other unit. The time it took to reach the meeting site is given as 1 hour 30 minutes. The time written as 1 hour 30 minutes cannot be used in the formula for speed shown above. The time must be one number in hours only. To convert 1 hour 30 minutes into hours only use the procedure below:

It is known that 1 hour is equivalent to 60 minutes. So in total, 1 hour 30 minutes is equivalent to 60 + 30 = 90 minutes

To convert 90 minutes into hours, divide it by 60 minutes as there are 60 minutes in 1 hour:

$$90 \text{ } \textit{minutes converted into hours} \text{ } = 90 \div 60$$

$$= 1.5 \textit{ hours}$$

There is also an alternative to this calculation. By knowing that 30 mins is half an hour it is possible to write 30 minutes as 0.5 hours. Then 1 hour 30 minutes becomes:

$$1 + 0.5 = 1.5 \textit{ hours}$$

This can now be plugged straight into the speed formula:

$$\textit{Speed} = \frac{120 \textit{ (miles)}}{1.5 \textit{ (hours)}} = 80 \textit{ mph (miles per hour)}$$

The answer to question 9 is **a)** 80 mph

QUESTION 10

Whilst driving you average 30 mph over 1 hour 20 minutes. What distance have you covered in this time?

a) 32 miles

b) 40 miles

c) 50 miles

d) 43 miles

e) 45 miles

ANSWER TO QUESTION 10

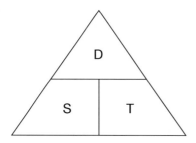

In the above triangle:

D represents Distance

S represents Speed

T represents Time.

If you want to calculate the distance, D, simply place your thumb over D on the triangle you will now see that D = S × T

The formula to use here is:

Distance (in miles) = speed (mph) × time (hours)

The speed is given in the question as 30 mph so this can be put straight into the formula as the units of mph match the units the formula needs to be in. The time is given as 1 hour 20 minutes. This is a combination of hours and minutes and in order to use this in the formula above it will have to be converted completely into hours.

1 hour 20 minutes = 80 minutes (because 1 hour = 60 minutes then add the 20 minutes to give 80 minutes)

To convert minutes into hours divide the minutes by 60 as there as 60 minutes in 1 hour.

80 minutes in hour's = 80 ÷ 60 = 1.333333.... hours

This can now be put straight into the distance formula as shown:

Distance (in miles) = *speed (mph)* × *time (hours)*

= 30 × 1.3333333....

= 40 miles

The answer is **b)** 40 miles

QUESTION 11

The heights of 10 random people are listed as 185 cm, 196 cm, 165 cm, 177 cm, 189 cm, 210 cm, 188 cm, 195 cm, 200 cm, 187 cm. What is the average height?

a) 190.2 cm

b) 189.2 cm

c) 173.5 cm

d) 182.6 cm

e) 191.8

ANSWER TO QUESTION 11

To find the average of any list of numbers add them all up together to get a total then divide by how many there are as shown below:

$$Average\ height = \frac{185 + 196 + 165 + 177 + 189 + 210 + 188 + 195 + 200 + 187}{10}$$

$$= \frac{1892}{10}$$

$$= 189.2cm$$

The answer is **b)** 189.2 cm

QUESTION 12

A garage is selling three used cars. The mileage on the first is 139,500, the mileage on the second is 120,500, and the mileage on the third is 160,000. What is the average mileage of the three used cars?

a) 140,000

b) 145,000

c) 150,000

d) 135,000

e) 130,000

ANSWER TO QUESTION 12

To find the average of a list of numbers add them all together then divide by how many there are. The average for this question can be calculated as follows:

$$\text{Average mileage} = \frac{\text{Total mileage for all 3 cars}}{3 \text{ cars}}$$

$$= \frac{139,500 + 120,500 + 160,000}{3}$$

$$= \frac{420,000}{3}$$

$$= 140,000$$

The answer is **a)** 140,000 is the average mileage of the three used cars.

QUESTION 13

Sam, Steve and Mark are brothers. Sam is 36, Steve is 28 and Mark is 26. What is their average age?

   a) 29

   b) 32

   c) 31

   d) 33

   e) 30

ANSWER TO QUESTION 13

To find the average of a list of numbers add them all together then divide by how many there are. The average age for this question can be calculated as follows:

$$\text{Average age} = \frac{\text{Total age for all 3 brothers}}{\text{Amount of brothers}}$$

$$= \frac{36 + 28 + 26}{3}$$

$$= \frac{90}{3}$$

$$= 30$$

The answer to question 13 is **e)** 30

QUESTION 14

There are four suspects in a police line up. Suspect A is 1.20m tall, suspect B is 1.25m tall, suspect C is 1.55m tall and suspect D is 1.6m tall. What is the average height of the suspects?

   a) 1.41m

   b) 1.40m

   c) 1.42m

   d) 1.39m

   e) 1.37m

ANSWER TO QUESTION 14

To find the average of a list of numbers add them all together then divide by how many there are. The average age for this question can be calculated as follows:

$$\text{Average height} = \frac{\textit{Total height for all 4 suspects}}{\textit{Number of suspects}}$$

$$= \frac{1.20 + 1.25 + 1.55 + 1.6}{4}$$

$$= \frac{5.6}{4}$$

$$= 1.40m$$

The answer to question 14 is **b)** 1.40 m

QUESTION 15

The perimeter of a training yard is 240 metres. The yard has a square perimeter. What is the average length of a side of the yard?

    a) 40 metres

    b) 50 metres

    c) 60 metres

    d) 120 metres

    e) 130 metres

ANSWER TO QUESTION 15

The question states that the yard has a square perimeter. This means that the yard has 4 sides, just like a square does. The total perimeter is 240 metres. To find the average length of a side of the yard divide 240 metres by 4:

$$Length\ of\ one\ side = 240 \div 4$$

$$= 60\ metres$$

If you didn't quite understand the above method, there is also another explanation. Below is an image of the yard. Let each side of the yard be *x metres* long.

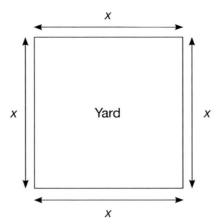

To calculate the perimeter of a square, add the lengths of all the sides together. So for the yard shown above, which is in the shape of a square, the total perimeter would be:

Total perimeter of the yard $= x + x + x + x$

$= 4x$

The question states that the total perimeter of the yard is 240 metres. I can substitute 240 metres into the above equation to find x, which is the length of one side of the yard as shown below:

Total perimeter of the yard $= 4x$

$240 \ metres = 4x$

$240 \div 4 = x$

$60 \ metres = x$

$x = 60 \ metres$ where x is the average length of a side of the yard.

The answer to question 15 is **c)** 60 metres

QUESTION 16

The police are escorting approximately 540 football fans to the train station. A train can carry 135 people. How many trains will be needed to transport the fans?

    a) 2

    b) 4

    c) 6

    d) 8

    e) 9

ANSWER TO QUESTION 16

There are 540 football fans. If one train can only carry 135 people then two trains will carry twice this amount i.e. 135 × 2 = 270 people and three trains will carry three times the amount of people one train carries i.e. 135 × 3 = 405 people. Clearly, 3 trains are not enough to carry the 540 football fans. So now try 4 trains. Four trains can carry four times the amount of people one train carries which is 135 × 4 = 540 people. Therefore 4 trains are enough to carry all 540 football fans.

Another way to work this out is to divide 540 by 135:

Amount of trains required to transport 540 *fans if each train can carry a maximum of* 135 *people*:

$$540 \div 135 = 4 \text{ } trains$$

The answer to question 16 is **b)** 4 trains are required to transport 540 football fans.

QUESTION 17

Darren commutes to and from work every day from Monday to Friday. His office is 40 miles away from his house. How many miles does Darren drive per week?

  a) 200

  b) 400

  c) 800

  d) 1,000

  e) 1,200

ANSWER TO QUESTION 17

The distance from Darren's house to his office is 40 miles away.
The distance from Darren's office to his house is also 40 miles.
In total, for Darren to get to work and back home every day he travels
40 + 40 = 80 *miles*

The question also states that Darren travels to his office and back home every day from Monday to Friday (5 days). To calculate the miles Darren does per week i.e. Monday to Friday simply multiply the miles he travels in one day (80 miles) by the number of days he travels (5 days):

$$\text{Miles Darren drives per week} = 80 \times 5$$

$$= 400 \text{ miles}$$

The answer to question 17 is **b)** 400

QUESTION 18

John runs a marathon (26 miles) with 69 other runners. Every single runner completes the marathon. What is the combined distance run by all the runners?

 a) 1784

 b) 1830

 c) 1794

 d) 1820

 e) 1824

ANSWER TO QUESTION 18

There are 70 runners in total (John + 69 other runners). All 70 runners complete the 26 mile marathon. To calculate the combined distance run by all the runners multiply 70 by 26:

Combined distance run by all the runners = 70 × 26

= 1820 miles

The answer to question 18 is **d)** 1820 miles

QUESTION 19

You bicycle for 2 hours at an average speed of 18 mph. What distance have you travelled in total?

a) 9 miles

b) 20 miles

c) 36 miles

d) 24 miles

e) 22 miles

ANSWER TO QUESTION 19

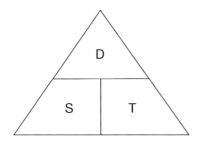

In the above triangle:

D represents Distance

S represents Speed

T represents Time.

If you wanted a formula to calculate distance D, simply place your thumb over D on the triangle. You will now see that D = S × T

The formula to use here is:

Distance (in miles) = speed (mph) × time (hours)

It is fine to put both speed and time straight into the formula for distance without having to convert anything into different units as speed is already in mph and time is already in hours.

Distance (in miles) = speed (mph) × time (hours)

= 18 *mph* × 2 *hours*

= 36 *miles*

The answer to question 19 is **c)** 36miles

QUESTION 20

You own a market stall and sell 216 apples. You have sold apples to 36 customers. On average how many apples did each customer buy?

a) 4

b) 6

c) 8

d) 12

e) 14

ANSWER TO QUESTION 20

To calculate the average, divide the total number of apples sold by the number of customers that bought them. This will give the average of how many apples each customer bought.

Average amount of apples each customer bought $= 216 \div 36$

$= 6$ *apples*

The answer to question 20 is **b)** 6

QUESTION 21

The Metropolitan Police have 1,200 police officers on duty. They want 300 areas patrolled. How many police officers should go on each patrol?

    a) 2

    b) 3

    c) 5

    d) 6

    e) 4

ANSWER TO QUESTION 21

There are 1,200 police officers and 300 areas to patrol. To find the number of police officers that should go on each patrol equally, divide the number of police officers by the number of areas to patrol.

Number of police officers on each patrol $= 1,200 \div 300$

$= 4$ *police officers*

This means that for one out of the 300 patrols there will be 4 officers.

The answer to question 21 is **e)** 4

QUESTION 22

A leisure complex has three pools: pool A, pool B and pool C. What is the area of swimming pool A?

a) 6 m²

b) 10 m²

c) 12 m²

d) 14 m²

e) 21 m²

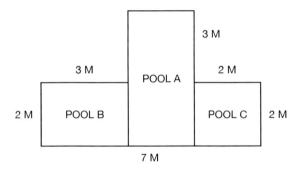

ANSWER TO QUESTION 22

The length of pools A, B and C combined is 7m. The question gives the length of pool B as 3m and pool C's length as 2m. The total length of pool's B and C combined is 3 + 2 = 5m. Therefore, the length of pool A must be the total length of all three pools A,B and C minus the lengths of pool's B and C combined:

$$\textit{Length of pool A} = 7 - 5$$

$$= 2m$$

To find the height of pool A, add the 3m given in the diagram which is the measurement from the top of pool A up to where pool's B and C begin to the 2m measurement which is measured from the top to the bottom of pools B and C.

$$\textit{The height of pool A} = 3 + 2$$

$$= 5m$$

To calculate the area of pool A, multiply the length of pool A by the height of pool A:

$$Area\ of\ pool\ A = 2m \times 5m$$

$$= 10m^2$$

The answer to question 22 is **b)** $10m^2$

QUESTION 23

What is the average weekly wage of a team of five people whose individual wages are: £59.00, £61.00, £64.00, £76.00 and £80.00?

   a) £64

   b) £68

   c) £73

   d) £76

   e) £77

ANSWER TO QUESTION 23

To calculate the average weekly wage sum all the weekly wages together and divide by how many people there are.

$$\text{Average weekly wage} = \frac{£59 + £61 + £64 + £76 + £80}{5}$$

$$= \frac{£340}{5}$$

$$= £68$$

The answer to question 23 is **b)** £68

QUESTION 24

Response times to Fire Brigade emergency calls vary throughout the week; on Monday it is 7 minutes, on Tuesday it's 7 minutes, on Wednesday it's 5 minutes, on Thursday it's 6 minutes, on Friday it's 9 minutes, on Saturday it's 8 minutes and finally on Sunday it's 7 minutes. What is the average response time?

   a) 6 minutes

   b) 5 minutes

   c) 8 minutes

   d) 9 minutes

   e) 7 minutes

ANSWER TO QUESTION 24

Add all the response times and then divide by how many response times there are to find the average response time:

$$Average\ response\ time = \frac{7 + 7 + 5 + 6 + 9 + 8 + 7}{7}$$

$$= \frac{49}{7}$$

$$= 7\ minutes$$

The answer to question 24 is **e)** 7 minutes

QUESTION 25

There are 7 new Police Officers at a Wolverhampton police station. Their ages are 18, 19, 21, 24, 28, 29 and 36. What is their average age?

    a) 22 years old

    b) 24 years old

    c) 25 years old

    d) 26 years old

    e) 27 years old

ANSWER TO QUESTION 25

To find the average age, add all the ages together then divide by how many police officers there are:

$$\text{Average age} = \frac{18 + 19 + 21 + 24 + 28 + 29 + 36}{7}$$

$$= \frac{175}{7}$$

$$= 25$$

The answer to question 25 is **c)** 25 years old

QUESTION 26

There are 150 guests at a Spanish holiday complex. 50 of the guests are British, 35 are German, 10 are French, and 5 are Italian. The rest of the guests are Spanish. What percentage of guests are Spanish?

a) 33.33%

b) 32%

c) 33%

d) 66.66%

e) 70%

ANSWER TO QUESTION 26

In total there are 150 guests. The question gives the number of people who are British, German, French and Italian but NOT Spanish. Therefore the number of Spanish guests will have to be calculated. This can be done by adding together all the guests who are not Spanish and subtracting from the total of 150 guests to leave the number of Spanish guests since the question states that the rest of the guests are Spanish.

Number of Spanish guests = 150 – (*British,German,French and Italian guests*)

$$= 150 - (50 + 35 + 10 + 5)$$

$$= 150 - 100$$

$$= 50 \ Spanish \ guests$$

Therefore, there are 50 Spanish guests out of 150 guests in total. To write this a percentage, divide 50 by 150 and multiply by 100 as shown:

$$\frac{50}{150} \times 100 = 33.33\%$$

This means that 33.33% of all guests are Spanish.

The answer to question 26 is **a)** 33.33%

QUESTION 27

A container ship carries 1,000 barrels. Each barrel contains 330 litres of oil. How much oil is contained in the barrels?

a) 330 litres

b) 3,300 litres

c) 33,000 litres

d) 330,000 litres

e) 3,300,000 litres

ANSWER TO QUESTION 27

Each barrel contains 330 litres of oil. Multiply this by 1,000 to find how much oil is contained in all the 1,000 barrels combined.

$$\textit{Oil contained in the barrels} = 330 \times 1000$$

$$= 330,000 \text{ litres}$$

The answer to question 27 is **d)** 330,000 litres

QUESTION 28

A bike company has 12 factories each producing 102 bikes a day. How many bikes does the company produce per day?

  a) 1,004

  b) 1,040

  c) 1,204

  d) 1,224

  e) 1,226

ANSWER TO QUESTION 28

Each factory produces 102 bikes a day and the company runs 12 of these factories.

Number of bikes the company produces per day $= 102 \times 12$

$= 1,224$ bikes

The answer to question 28 is **d)** 1,224 bikes

QUESTION 29

In a biscuit tin there are 28 biscuits. If you were to divide these equally between a family of 4, how many biscuits would each family member get?

a) 7

b) 4

c) 8

d) 3.5

e) 5

ANSWER TO QUESTION 29

28 biscuits are to be shared by 4 people. The calculation is as follows:

$$\frac{28}{4} = 7 \text{ biscuits each}$$

The answer to question 29 is **a)** 7

QUESTION 30

A plane can carry a maximum of 180 passengers. There are 36 rows on the plane. How many passengers are there on each row assuming the plane is full?

a) 9

b) 6

c) 7

d) 8

e) 5

ANSWER TO QUESTION 30

To find the number of passengers on each row simply divide the total amount of passengers by the amount of rows on the plane.

$$Number\ of\ passengers\ on\ each\ row = \frac{180}{36} = 5\ people$$

The answer to question 30 is **e)** 5 people

QUESTION 31

You have been driving for 2 hours 15 minutes at a constant speed of 48 mph. How far have you driven so far?

   a) 180 miles

   b) 108 miles

   c) 104 miles

   d) 140 miles

   e) 144 miles

ANSWER TO QUESTION 31

This question is asking you to calculate a distance.

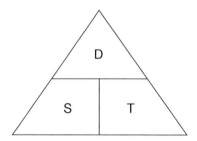

In the above triangle:

D represents Distance

S represents Speed

T represents Time.

If you wanted a formula to calculate distance D, simply place your thumb over D on the triangle. You will now see that $D = S \times T$

The formula to use here is:

Distance (in miles) = speed (mph) × time (hours)

The first thing that needs to be done before the above formula can be used is to convert 2 hours 15 minutes into hours only.

The quickest way this can be done is by knowing that 15 minutes is a quarter of an hour and a quarter of an hour in decimal form is 0.25 hours i.e. 1/4 = 0.25. Therefore, 15 minutes equals 0.25 hours so 2 hours 15 mins is equivalent to 2.25 hours i.e. (2 *hours* + 0.25 *hours* = 2.25 *hours*).

If you didn't know that 15 minutes is equal to 0.25 hours there is an alternative. In case you get stuck always use the method shown below to convert minutes into hours.

ALTERNATIVE METHOD

1 hour is 60 minutes. Therefore, 2 hours is double this which is 120 minutes. Now add the 15 minutes to this and it becomes clear that 2 hours 15 minutes is equivalent to 135 minutes.

To convert minutes into hours, divide by 60 as there are 60 minutes in 1 hour:

$$Converting\ 135\ minutes\ into\ hours = 135 \div 60$$

$$= 2.25\ hours$$

$$Distance\ (in\ miles) = speed\ (mph) \times time\ (hours)$$

$$= 48 \times 2.25$$

$$= 108\ miles$$

The answer to question 31 is **b)** 108 miles

QUESTION 32

A sprinter runs 200 metres in 22 seconds. How long would it take him to run 2,000 metres if he continued to run at the same speed?

a) 3 minutes 40 seconds

b) 3 minutes 20 seconds

c) 4 minutes 20 seconds

d) 3 minutes 15 seconds

e) 4 minutes 15 seconds

ANSWER TO QUESTION 32

This question is asking you to calculate a time.

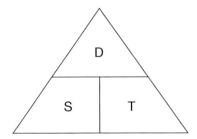

In the above triangle:

D represents Distance

S represents Speed

T represents Time.

If you wanted a formula to calculate time, T, simply place your thumb over T on the triangle. You will now see that $T = D \div S$

The formula to use here is:

> *Time (in seconds) = distance(metres) ÷ speed (metres per second)*

Notice how the units have changed according to the nature of the question. All units used in the question were either seconds or metres. In previous questions we have seen the use of miles and hours. Remember to vary the units you use according to the question.

The sprinters does 200 metres in 22 seconds. From this information alone it is possible to calculate the sprinters speed. Using the formula:

$$speed = distance \div time$$

$$= 200 \ metres \div 22 \ seconds$$

$$= 9.090909.....metres \ per \ second$$

The question then asks how long it would take the sprinter to run 2,000 metres at this speed. This can now be calculated using the above formula for time.

$$Time \ (in \ seconds) = distance(metres) \div speed \ (metres \ per \ second)$$

$$= 2,000 \ metres \div 9.090909 \ metres \ per \ second$$

$$= 220 \ seconds$$

Because there are 60 seconds in 1 minute, 220 seconds is 3 minutes and 40 seconds.

The answer to question 32 is **a)** 3 minutes 40 seconds

QUESTION 33

Samantha is a carpenter. She makes 3 oak tables for a family. The first table top measures 0.75 x 2 metres, the second measures 1.5 x 3 metres and the third measures 1.0 x 3 metres. What is the average area of the table tops?

a) 5 m²

b) 4 m²

c) 3 m²

d) 2 m²

e) 2.5 m²

ANSWER TO QUESTION 33

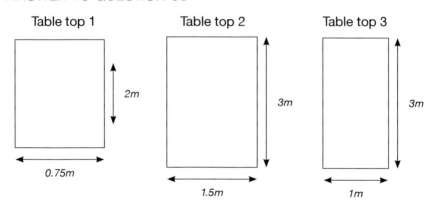

Table top 1   Table top 2   Table top 3

2m   3m   3m

0.75m   1.5m   1m

Area of table top 1   Area of table top 2   Area of table top 3

= 0.75 m × 2 m   = 1.5 m × 3 m   = 1 m × 3 m

= 1.5 m²   = 4.5m²   = 3m²

To find the average area of all 3 table tops, add all the areas together and divide by the amount of tables there are:

$$\text{Average area of the table tops} = \frac{1.5m^2 + 4.5m^2 + 3m^2}{3}$$

$$= \frac{9m^2}{3}$$

$$= 3m^2$$

The answer to question 33 is **c)** $3m^2$

QUESTION 34

Five students buy a pizza each. Each pizza costs £5.20. The students are each given 10% discount. What is the total bill for the students?

a) £23.20

b) £23.40

c) £23.60

d) £24.40

e) £24.60

ANSWER TO QUESTION 34

Each pizza costs £5.20 but students receive a 10% discount off this price. The price a student pays for one pizza can therefore be calculated as shown below:

Useful tips:

- In mathematics, the word 'of' means multiply
- 10% means 10 out of 100. To write 10% as a decimal or a fraction, divide 10 by 100 (10% = 10/100 = 0.1)

METHOD 1

Find 10% of £5.20 and then subtract this from £5.20.

$$10\% \text{ } of \text{ } £5.20 = 0.1 \times £5.20$$

$$= £0.52$$

This means that every student buying a pizza gets 52 pence off the normal price of £5.20.

The students therefore pay: £5.20 – £0.52 = £4.68 each for one pizza.

METHOD 2

The normal price for a pizza is £5.20. This is 100% of the price of a pizza therefore a 10% discount would mean that the students pay (100%-10% = 90%) of the £5.20 price.

Remember that 90% is the same as 90 out of 100, which equals 0.9

Price each student pays for a pizza after a 10% discount = £5.20 × 90%

= £5.20 × 0.9

= £4.68

The students pay £4.68 for a pizza after a 10% discount using both methods 1 and 2. You can use the method which you find easiest to work with as both lead to the same answers.

The total bill for all 5 students will be the price of one pizza after a 10% discount multiplied by 5.

Total bill = £4.68 × 5

= £23.40

The answer to question 34 is **b)** £23.40

QUESTION 35

At a campsite there are 240 tents. During a flood, 2.5% of the tents are damaged. How many tents were damaged during the flood?

a) 6

b) 8

c) 5

d) 9

e) 4

ANSWER TO QUESTION 35

Firstly, convert 2.5% into a decimal. Dividing 2.5% by 100 will do this:

$$\frac{2.5\%}{100} = 0.025$$

2.5% of 240 tents are damaged. Remember that in mathematics the word 'of' means multiply.

$$Number\ of\ tents\ damaged = 2.5\% \times 240$$

$$= 0.025 \times 240$$

$$= 6\ tents$$

The answer to question 35 is **a)** 6 tents were damaged during the flood.

QUESTION 36

36. In your savings account there is £13,000. You decide to withdraw 40% to buy a car. How much money do you withdraw?

    a) £520

    b) £5,200

    c) £7,200

    d) £8,000

    e) £8,200

ANSWER TO QUESTION 36

40% of £13,000 is withdrawn. Once again remember that of in mathematics means multiply. Also, 40% written as a decimal is 40/100 = 0.4

$$Amount\ withdrawn = 40\% \times £13,000$$

$$= 0.4 \times £13,000$$

$$= £5,200$$

The answer to question 36 is **b)** £5,200

QUESTION 37

You own a Ford Fiesta which is currently worth £8000. Since you bought the car it has depreciated in value by 30% of its original value. How much was the original value of the vehicle?

   a) £8,242

   b) £11,429

   c) £10,450

   d) £12,429

   e) £12,450

ANSWER TO QUESTION 37

Let x be the original value of the vehicle. It has depreciated by 30% since to make the current value £8,000.

If a value depreciates by 30% this means that it only has 100% − 30% = 70% remaining of its original value.

This can be written as: $x \times 70\% = £8000$

Where x is the original value of the vehicle.

Remember that 70% = 70/100 = 0.7

Use the following method to find x, the original value of the vehicle:

$$x \times 0.7 = £8000$$

$$x = \frac{£8000}{0,7}$$

$$x = £11428.57$$

$$x = £11,429$$

The answer to question 37 is **b)** £11,429

QUESTION 38

A ticket for a football match costs £12. If 12,000 people go to the game, how much in total will ticket sales make?

   a) £14,400

   b) £144,000

   c) £288,000

   d) £144,0000

   e) £420,000

ANSWER TO QUESTION 38

Each ticket costs £12 per person. If there are 12,000 people going to a game simply multiply £12 by 12,000 to find the total ticket sales in pounds.

$$\textit{Total ticket sales} = 12{,}000 \times £12$$

$$= £144{,}000$$

Be careful not to select the wrong answer to this question. The correct answer has 3 zeros at the end of the number.

The answer to question 38 is **b)** £144,000

QUESTION 39

A solicitor charges £28 per hour for legal services. If you hired a solicitor for 12 hours, how much would you be charged?

    a) £326

    b) £336

    c) £374

    d) £436

    e) £442

ANSWER TO QUESTION 39

To calculate how much you would be charged if you hired a solicitor for 12 hours at a rate of £28 per hour, simply multiply the price of the solicitor per hour by the number of hours you hired the solicitor as shown below.

Charge for hiring a solicitor for 12 *hours* = £28 × 12

= £336

The answer to question 39 is **b)** £336

QUESTION 40

At a grammar school there are 200 students. 15 of the students get straight A's. What is this as a percentage?

a) 7.5%

b) 10%

c) 15%

d) 30%

e) 45%

ANSWER TO QUESTION 40

Out of a total of 200 students at the grammar school, 15 got an A grade. As a fraction this can be expressed as:

$$15 \; out \; of \; 200 = 15/200$$

There are two ways of now finding this as a percentage.

METHOD 1:

A percentage is defined as 'out of 100'. Currently, the fraction 15/200 is out of 200. This is twice the amount we need it to be to calculate a percentage. Therefore, halve the numerator (top half of the fraction) and the denominator (lower half of the fraction) to give:

$$\frac{15}{200} \; \overset{\div 2}{\underset{\div 2}{=}} \; \frac{7.5}{100}$$

7.5 is now out of 100. To convert a fraction into a percentage, simply multiply it by 100%.

$$\frac{7.5}{100} \times 100\% = 7.5\%$$

METHOD 2

Using a calculator, calculate 15/200 × 100% = 7.5%

The answer to question 40 is **a)** 7.5%

QUESTION 41

You find a missing wallet in the street. It contains a £10 note, two £5 notes, three £1 coins, a 50p coin and six 2p coins. How much is in the wallet?

a) £22.72

b) £22.62

c) £24.62

d) £23.56

e) £23.62

ANSWER TO QUESTION 41

It is best to make a list of all the different coins in the wallet and the amount of those coins that were in the wallet as shown below.

$$1 \times £10 = £10$$

$$2 \times £5 = £10$$

$$3 \times £1 = £3$$

$$1 \times 50p = 50p$$

$$6 \times 2p = 12p$$

$$Total = £23.62$$

The answer to question 41 is **e)** £23.62

QUESTION 42

Your car does 35 miles to the gallon. The car takes 8 gallons of petrol full. If you were to drive 560 miles how much petrol would you need?

a) 12 gallon

b) 14 gallons

c) 16 gallons

d) 18 gallons

e) 24 gallons

ANSWER TO QUESTION 42

This question has given you an extra bit of information: "The car takes 8 gallons of petrol full", which is not necessarily required to solve the question. However, this model answer will show you how to solve this question both using this bit of information and without using it.

Solving question 42 using the extra bit of information

For every 35 miles the car travels it uses up 1 gallon of petrol. If the same car takes 8 gallons of petrol to fill it can travel 35 × 8 = 280 *miles*.

Another way to work this out if you are unsure is to use the cross multiplication method as shown:

Let the miles travelled when 8 gallons are used be *x*

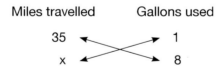

Miles travelled   Gallons used

Cross multiplying gives the following equation:

$$35 \times 8 = 1 \times x$$

Remember that x is the miles travelled when the car is filled with 8 gallons of petrol and it is the quantity that needs to be found from the above equation.

$$x = \frac{35 \times 8}{1} = 280 \ people$$

Therefore the car can drive 280 miles using 8 gallons. However the question asks for how many gallons of petrol is required when travelling 560 miles.

Once again, use the cross multiplication method. Let y be the gallons of petrol required to cover 560 miles by car:

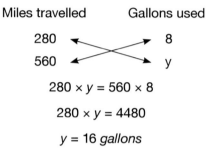

Miles travelled   Gallons used

280   8

560   y

$$280 \times y = 560 \times 8$$

$$280 \times y = 4480$$

$$y = 16 \ gallons$$

It therefore takes 16 gallons of petrol to travel 560 miles using the car.

*Solving question 42 **without** using the extra bit of information*

Using cross multiplication again, the question states that 1 gallon allows the car to drive 35 miles. How many gallons would it need to travel 560 miles?

Let y be the amount of gallons required to travel 560 miles

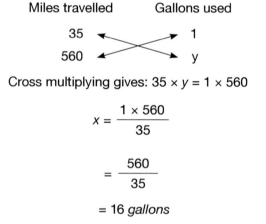

Miles travelled   Gallons used

35   1

560   y

Cross multiplying gives: $35 \times y = 1 \times 560$

$$x = \frac{1 \times 560}{35}$$

$$= \frac{560}{35}$$

$$= 16 \ gallons$$

Therefore the car needs 16 gallons to travel 560 miles and the answer to question 43 is **c)** 16 gallons

QUESTION 43

Two farmers, Jack and Tom, both own adjoining fields. What is the total combined area of both Jack's and Tom's fields?

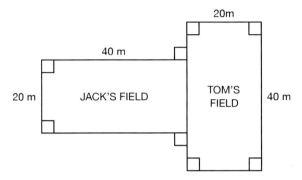

a) 160m²

b) 240m²

c) 800m²

d) 1600m²

e) 2400m²

ANSWER TO QUESTION 43

Start by calculating one field's area out of the two and then calculate the other fields area and finally add them together to get the total combined area of both Jack and Tom's fields.

$$Area\ of\ Jack's\ field = 40 \times 20$$

$$= 800m^2$$

$$Area\ of\ Tom's\ field = 20 \times 40$$

$$= 800m^2$$

The total combined area of both fields can be found by adding up the individual area of both Jack's and Tom's fields.

$$Total\ combined\ area = 800m^2 + 800m^2$$

$$= 1600m^2$$

The answer to question 43 is **d)** 1600m²

QUESTION 44

A school has 15 classes with 23 students in each class. How many students are at the school?

    a) 245

    b) 325

    c) 335

    d) 445

    e) 345

ANSWER TO QUESTION 44

If there are 15 classes each with 23 students, the total amount of students at the school can be found by multiplying the number of classes with the number of students.

$$Number\ of\ students\ at\ the\ school = 15 \times 23$$

$$= 345\ students$$

The answer to question 44 is **e)** 345 students

QUESTION 45

A restaurant serves 60 customers a night. If on average each customer spends £30, what is the total average for the night?

    a) £180

    b) £1,600

    c) £2,400

    d) £1,800

    e) £1,260

ANSWER TO QUESTION 45

If there are 60 customers and each customer spends £30 on average simply multiply the number of customers by the average spend per customer to get the total average spent for the night.

$$\textit{Total average for the night} = 60 \times £30$$

$$= £1,800$$

The answer to question 45 is **d)** £1,800

QUESTION 46

A chocolate bar costs 59p. If you were to buy 6 chocolate bars, how much would it cost you?

> **a)** £3.34

> **b)** £3.45

> **c)** £3.54

> **d)** £4.24

> **e)** £4.14

ANSWER TO QUESTION 46

If one chocolate bar costs 59p then 6 would cost 6 times this amount.

$$Cost\ of\ 6\ chocolate\ bars\ (59p\ each) = 59 \times 6$$

$$= 354p$$

$$= £3.54$$

Remember that if you start the calculation in pence, it will end in pence. This is why the answer is 354 p. To convert this into pounds divide by 100 as 100 pence equals 1 pound to get an answer of £3.54

The answer to question 46 is **c)** £3.54

QUESTION 47

You fly a three-leg journey in a light aircraft. The total distance covered is 270 miles. What is the average distance of each leg?

a) 70 miles

b) 80 miles

c) 90 miles

d) 135 miles

e) 140 miles

ANSWER TO QUESTION 47

To find the average distance of each leg, divide the total distance covered which in this case is 270 miles by 3 as it was a three-leg journey as shown below:

$$\textit{Average distance of each leg} = \frac{270}{3}$$

$$= 90 \ \textit{miles}$$

The answer to question 47 is **c)** 90 miles

QUESTION 48

On average a bank repossesses 3 out of 150 homes every year. The village of Claxby has 1,000 homes. Under the above principle, how many homes would be repossessed in the village?

    a) 10

    b) 15

    c) 20

    d) 25

    e) 30

ANSWER TO QUESTION 48

This means that for every 150 homes there are 3 that are possessed i.e. 3/150 are repossessed. To calculate the amount of homes that would be repossessed in the village of Claxby according to the 3 out of 150 homes repossessed principle, it would be necessary to multiply 3/150 by 1000.

You can think of 3/150 being the scale factor and using this you can work out the amount of any homes that would be repossessed, simply by multiplying with this scale factor. For this question, there are 1000 homes so multiply by 1000 as shown below:

$$\textit{Homes repossessed in the village} = \frac{3}{150} \times 1{,}000 = 20 \textit{ homes}$$

The answer to question 48 is **c)** 20

QUESTION 49

A team of 12 explorers find the wreck of a ship. The ship contains 6 gold bars each worth £120,000. How much money does each team member make?

　a) £40,000

　b) £60,000

　c) £100,000

　d) £120,000

　e) £130,000

ANSWER TO QUESTION 49

There are 6 gold bars each worth £120,000 so in total the entire value of all 6 gold bars would be:

$$\textit{Value of all 6 gold bars combined} = 6 \times £120,000$$

$$= £720,000$$

There are a team of 12 explorers that share the combined value of all 6 gold bars which is £720,000.

To calculate how much each explorer gets, divide £720,000 by 12:

$$\textit{Amount each explorer makes} = \frac{£720,000}{12} = £60,000$$

Therefore, each explorer makes £60,000

The answer to question 49 is **b)** £60,000

QUESTION 50

A magazine contains 110 pages. If you bought seven magazines, how many pages are there in total?

    a) 700

    b) 720

    c) 740

    d) 770

    e) 780

ANSWER TO QUESTION 50

If one magazine contains 110 pages, then 7 magazines would contain 7 times this.

$$Total\ pages\ in\ 7\ magazines = 110 \times 7$$

$$= 770$$

The answer to question 50 is **d)** 770

QUESTION 51

A car is travelling at 72 miles per hour. How many miles will it have travelled in 45 minutes?

   a) 54

   b) 52

   c) 50

   d) 48

   e) 46

ANSWER TO QUESTION 51

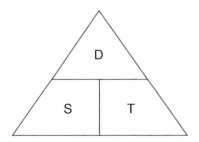

In the above triangle:

D represents Distance

S represents Speed

T represents Time.

If you wanted a formula to calculate distance, D, simply place your thumb over D on the triangle. You will now see that $D = S \times T$

The formula to use here is:

Distance (in miles) − speed (mph) × time (hours)

The first thing that needs to be done is to convert 45 minutes into hours. This can be achieved by dividing 45 by 60:

$$45 \text{ minutes in hours} = \frac{45}{60} = 0.75 \text{ homes}$$

You may have heard the expression 'three quarters of an hour' when people are referring to 45 minutes. The reason for this is that 0.75 hours as a fraction is equivalent to 3/4 (three quarters).

It is now possible to use the distance formula:

$$Distance\ (in\ miles) = speed\ (mph) \times time\ (hours)$$

$$= 72\ mph \times 0.75\ hours$$

$$= 54\ miles$$

The answer to question 51 is **a)** 54 miles

QUESTION 52

If carpet costs £1.20 per metre, how much will 35 metres of carpet cost?

a) £45.00

b) £43.75

c) £44.00

d) £46.75

e) £42.00

ANSWER TO QUESTION 52

1 metre of carpet costs £1.20. To calculate how much 35 metres will cost, simply multiply the cost of a 1 metre carpet by 35.

Cost of a 35 metre carpet = £1.20 × 35

= £42

The answer to question 52 is **e)** £42

SECTION 2
PRACTICE TESTS

Calculators allowed.

Aim to complete each practice test within 30 minutes.

PRACTICE TEST 1

Q1. If 70% of £500 has been spent, how much money remains?

    a. £125   **b.** £130   **c.** £140   **d.** £150   **e.** £160

Q2. A multi-storey office has 7 floors, and each floor has 49 employees. How many members of staff work in the multi-storey office?

    a. 257   **b.** 343   **c.** 357   **d.** 423   **e.** 475

Q3. Following some road works on the M1 the Highways Agency need their 5 vehicles to collect 1,250 cones. If each vehicle collects the same amount of cones, how many cones does each individual vehicle collect?

    a. 125   **b.** 200   **c.** 250   **d.** 500   **e.** 525

Q4. Laura buys three items: a pair of shoes, a dress, and a coat. The items totalled £340. If the shoes were £59.99 and the coat was £139.99, how much was the dress?

    a. £138.02   **b.** £138.00   **c.** £140.02   **d.** £142.00   **e.** £144.00

Q5. At Telford school there are 200 school students. 25 students get straight A's. What is this as a percentage?

    a. 12.5%   **b.** 10%   **c.** 15%   **d.** 30%   **e.** 25%

Q6. A carton of milk costs £1.19. How much change would you have left from £5.00 if you bought one carton?

    a. £2.81   **b.** £3.61   **c.** £3.71   **d.** £3.81   **e.** £4.05

Q7. You are driving down a motorway at 108 mph. How far do you travel in 25 minutes?

    a. 47 miles   **b.** 45 miles   **c.** 44 miles   **d.** 42 miles   **e.** 41 miles

Q8. A fast jet is flying at a speed of 270 mph. The distance from airfield A to airfield B is 90 miles. How long does it take to fly from A to B?

    a. 20 minutes   **b.** 24 minutes   **c.** 22 minutes
    d. 26 minutes   **e.** 28 minutes

Q9. You are travelling down a motorway. Your journey has lasted 50 minutes and you have covered 125 miles. What speed have you been travelling at?

    a. 162 mph   **b.** 155 mph   **c.** 160 mph   **d.** 152 mph   **e.** 150 mph

Q10. The AA on average responds to 25 calls a day. How many do they respond to in a week?

    a. 160   **b.** 165   **c.** 170   **d.** 175   **e.** 180

Q11. Lincolnshire, Yorkshire and Lancashire all have new police helicopters. It takes the Lincolnshire helicopter 15 minutes to fly to Leeds, the Lancashire helicopter takes 35 minutes and the Yorkshire helicopter takes 10 minutes. What is the average time it takes these three helicopters to get to Leeds?

    a. 15 minutes   **b.** 20 minutes   **c.** 25 minutes
    d. 30 minutes   **e.** 35 minutes

Q12. A car park has 500 available spaces. On a busy day 75% of these are full.

How many full car parking spaces are there on a busy day?

    a. 375   **b.** 350   **c.** 325   **d.** 320   **e.** 310

Q13. You have £50 in your wallet and spend 70% of it on shopping. How much money have you spent on shopping?

    a. £30   **b.** £35   **c.** £40   **d.** £50   **e.** £45

Q14. The RSPCA has 120,000 officers. 3% of these officers are due to retire. How many officers will retire?

    a. 360,000   **b.** 36,000   **c.** 360   **d.** 36   **e.** 3,600

Q15. The road tax for your car cost £120 in 2007. In 2008 it increases by 10%. How much is the road tax in 2008?

    a. £121.20   **b.** £132   **c.** £142   **d.** £152   **e.** £152.20

Q16. A school decides to buy 12 laptops costing £850 each. What is the combined cost for the 12 laptops?

    a. £10,200   **b.** £10,400   **c.** £10,500   **d.** £10,600   **e.** £10,800

Q17. A metre of wool costs 62p. How much would it cost to buy 6 metres of wool?

    a. £3.72   **b.** £3.62   **c.** £3.82   **d.** £4.72   **e.** £5.12

Q18. Sally is riding her horse in a cross country competition. She has been told that she has to complete the course in 2 hours and 30 minutes. If divided into equal quarters, how long should she aim to spend completing each phase?

    a. 35 minutes   **b.** 37.5 minutes   **c.** 35.5 minutes
    d. 38.5 minutes **e.** 39.5 minutes

Q19. There are 18 teams entered in a rugby competition. If there are 6 changing rooms, how many teams use each changing room?

    a. 2   **b.** 4   **c.** 6   **d.** 3   **e.** 5

Q20. Using the diagram below, calculate the perimeter of the inner rectangle?

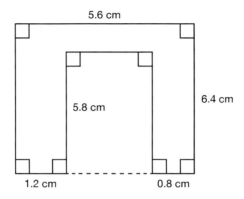

5.6 cm

6.4 cm

5.8 cm

1.2 cm   0.8 cm

    a. 16.4 cm   **b.** 17.2 cm   **c.** 17.8 cm   **d.** 18.4 cm   **e.** 18.8 cm

Q21. A room measures 20m by 5m. If I wanted to carpet 50% of it and I had 60 square metres of carpet available, how many square metres would I have left after finishing the task?

    a. 5m^2 **b.** 10m^2 **c.** 15m^2 **d.** 20m^2 **e.** 25m^2

Q22. If a ferry journey of 490 miles takes 7 hours, what is the average speed of

the ferry?

    a. 55 mph   **b.** 60 mph   **c.** 65 mph   **d.** 70 mph   **e.** 80 mph

Q23. A multi-storey car park has 8 levels. Each level has 111 car parking spaces. How many cars will be in the car park when it is full?

    a. 784   **b.** 888   **c.** 988   **d.** 8,888   **e.** 9,988

Q24. The office sweepstake wins £1,500. If this is divided by 25 employees, how much does each employee win?

    a. £30   **b.** £40   **c.** £60   **d.** £80   **e.** £85

ANSWERS TO PRACTICE TEST 1

ANSWER TO QUESTION 1 (PRACTICE TEST 1):

The word 'of' means multiply in mathematics.

Therefore 70% of £500 = 70% × £500

To calculate this, first convert 70% into a decimal. Any percentage can be converted into a decimal by dividing it by 100.

$$70\% = 70 \div 100 = 0.7$$

$$70\% \times £500 = 0.7 \times £500$$

$$= £350$$

This means that £350 has been spent. The remaining money, out of £500 can be found by subtracting the money spent (£350) from £500.

$$Money\ remaining = £500 - £350$$

$$= £150$$

The answer to question 1 (Practice test 1) is **d.** £150

ANSWER TO QUESTION 2 (PRACTICE TEST 1):

If there are 7 floors and on each floor there are 49 employees, then in total there must by:

$$Total\ number\ of\ staff\ in\ the\ multi\text{-}storey\ office = 49 \times 7$$

$$= 343$$

The answer to question 2 (Practice test 1) is **b.** 343

ANSWER TO QUESTION 3 (PRACTICE TEST 1):

There are 1,250 cones and only 5 vehicles to collect them all. If each vehicle collects the same amount of cones then this means that the number of cones are split equally between all 5 vehicles. Therefore to calculate how many cones each individual vehicle collects simply divide the total amount of cones by the number of vehicles:

$$Amount\ of\ cones\ each\ vehicle\ collects = 1,250 \div 5 = 250\ cones$$

The answer to question 3 (Practice test 1) is **c.** 250

ANSWER TO QUESTION 4 (PRACTICE TEST 1):

If all 3 items totalled £340, then simply subtract the price of the two items that you already know to leave the price of a dress, which equals £140.02 as shown below.

The total cost of buying all three items is £340. This can be written in an equation form as shown below.

Price of Pair of shoes + Price of Dress + Price of coat = £340

To find how much the dress was, the equation can be rearranged so that:

Price of Dress = £340 – *Price of Pair of Shoes* – *Price of coat*

Now the price of shoes and the price of a coat can be put into the above equation:

Price of Dress = £340 – £59.99 – £139.99

= £140.02

The answer to question 4 (Practice test 1) is **c.** £140.02

ANSWER TO QUESTION 5 (PRACTICE TEST 1):

Out of 200 school students, 25 of them get A's. As a fraction this can be written as:

$$\frac{25}{200}$$

It is important to now recall that percentages are always out of 100. The fraction above is currently out of 200. If the lower half of the fraction is divided by 2, then the fraction will be out of 100 as shown below:

$$\frac{25}{200} \overset{\div 2}{\underset{\div 2}{=}} \frac{12.5}{100}$$

To convert a fraction that is out of 100 into a percentage simply multiply it by 100 as shown below:

$$\frac{12.5}{100} \times \cancel{100}\% = 12.5\%$$

Note that the 100 from the lower half (denominator) of the fraction cancels with the 100 that is used to multiply the fraction with to leave 12.5%

The answer to question 5 (Practice test 1) is **a.** 12.5%

ANSWER TO QUESTION 6 (PRACTICE TEST 1):

There are two methods of calculating change. One is to count up and the other is to count down.

Method 1 (The count up method)

The carton of milk costs £1.19. I have £5. To work out how much change I would get I count up from £1.19 until I get to £5.

So, £1.19 add another £3 would give:

$$£1.19 + £3 = £4.19$$

This does not yet add up to £5 in total, so I know that I am due more change than £3. I can get from £4.19 to £5 by adding 81p. In total, I have needed to add £3.81 to £1.19 in order to make £5.

This means that the change I should get from £5 if a carton of milk costs £1.19 is £3.81

Method 2 (The countdown method)

The change can also be calculated by simply subtracting the cost of the product from the amount of money used to pay for it. So if I were to give £5 to the cashier when paying for a product that cost £1.19, the change would be calculated as shown below:

$$Change = £5 - £1.19$$

$$= £3.81$$

The answer to question 6 (Practice test 1) is **d.** £3.81

ANSWER TO QUESTION 7 (PRACTICE TEST 1):

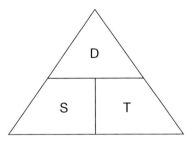

In the above triangle:

D represents Distance

S represents Speed

T represents Time.

If you wanted a formula to calculate distance D, simply place your thumb over D on the triangle. You will now see that $D = S \times T$

The formula to use here is:

Distance (in miles) = speed (mph) × time (hours)

The first thing that needs to be done is to convert 25 minutes into hours. This can be achieved by dividing 25 by 60:

$$25 \text{ minutes in hours} = \frac{25}{60} = 0.416666 \text{ hours}$$

It is now possible to use the distance formula:

Distance (in miles) = speed (mph) × time (hours)

= 108 mph × 0.416666 hours

= 45 miles

The answer to question 7 (Practice test 1) is **b.** 45 miles

ANSWER TO QUESTION 8 (PRACTICE TEST 1):

This question is asking you to calculate a time.

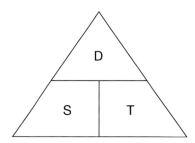

In the above triangle:

D represents Distance

S represents Speed

T represents Time.

If you wanted a formula to calculate time, T, simply place your thumb over T on the triangle. You will now see that $T = D \div S$

The formula to use here is:

Time (in hours) = distance(miles) ÷ speed (miles per hour)

= 90 miles ÷ 270 mph

= 0.333333 hours

To find what 0.3333 hours is in minutes, multiply 0.33333 hours by 60 as there are 60 minutes in 1 hour.

0.333333 hours × 60 = 20 minutes

The answer to question 8 (Practice test 1) is **a.** 20 minutes

ANSWER TO QUESTION 9 (PRACTICE TEST 1):

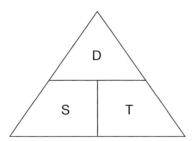

If you wanted a formula to calculate speed, simply place your thumb over S on the triangle. You will now see that S = D/T

The formula to use here is:

$$Speed\ (mph) = \frac{distance\ (miles)}{time\ (hour)}$$

The question gives the distance as 125 miles. Miles are the correct units to use for the formula and therefore 125 miles can be put straight into the formula without converting it to any other unit. The journey time is given as 50 minutes. The time written as 50 minutes cannot be used in the formula for speed shown above. The time in minutes must be converted into hours before it can be used in the above formula. To convert 50 minutes into hours only use the procedure below:

To convert 50 minutes into hours, divide it by 60 minutes as there are 60 minutes in 1 hour:

$$50\ minutes\ converted\ into\ hours = 50 \div 60$$

$$= 0.83333\ hours$$

This can now be used in the formula for speed:

$$Speed\ (mph) = \frac{125\ (miles)}{0.8333\ (hours)} = 150\ mph$$

The answer to question 9 (Practice test 1) is **e.** 150 mph

ANSWER TO QUESTION 10 (PRACTICE TEST 1):

There are 7 days in a week. If the AA responds to 25 calls a day, then to find how many calls they respond to in a week multiply 25 by 7.

Calls responded to in a week = 25 × 7 = 175

The answer to question 10 (Practice test 1) is **d.** 175

ANSWER TO QUESTION 11 (PRACTICE TEST 1):

An average is calculated by adding together all the individual times it took each helicopter to fly to Leeds and dividing by how many helicopters there are.

$$Average\ time = (15 + 35 + 10) \div 3$$

$$= 60 \div 3$$

$$= 20\ minutes$$

The answer to question 11 (Practice test 1) is **b.** 20 minutes

ANSWER TO QUESTION 12 (PRACTICE TEST 1):

75% of the 500 available spaces are full on a busy day. The word 'of' in mathematics means multiply. Therefore, to calculate 75% of 500 convert 75% into a decimal and then multiply it by 500. This will give the amount of full car parking spaces on a 'busy' day.

Step 1: Convert 75% into a decimal. To convert a percentage into a decimal, divide the percentage by 100:

$$75\% = 75 \div 100$$

$$= 0.75$$

Step 2: Multiply 500 by 0.75 to find how many parking spaces are full on a busy day:

$$500 \times 0.75 = 375$$

The answer to question 12 (Practice test 1) is **a.** 375 parking spaces were full on a busy day.

ANSWER TO QUESTION 13 (PRACTICE TEST 1):

This question states that you spent 70% of the £50 in your wallet. The word 'of' in mathematics means multiply and therefore the same method used to solve question 12 can be used here.

Step 1: Convert 70% into a decimal. To convert a percentage into a decimal, divide the percentage by 100:

$$70\% = 70 \div 100$$

$$= 0.70$$

Step 2: Multiply £50 by 0.75 to find how much money was spent on shopping:

$$£50 \times 0.70 = £35$$

The answer to question 13 (Practice test 1) is **b.** £35 was spent on shopping.

ANSWER TO QUESTION 14 (PRACTICE TEST 1):

This question states that 3% of the 120,000 officers in the RSPCA are due to retire. The word 'of' in mathematics means multiply and therefore the same method used to solve questions 12 and 13 can be used here.

Step 1: Convert 3% into a decimal. To convert a percentage into a decimal, divide the percentage by 100:

$$3\% = 3 \div 100$$

$$= 0.03$$

Step 2: Multiply 120,000 (the amount of officers in the RSPCA) by 0.03 to find how many officers will retire:

$$120,000 \times 0.03 = 3,600$$

The answer to question 14 (Practice test 1) is **e.** 3,600 officers are due to retire from the RSPCA.

ANSWER TO QUESTION 15 (PRACTICE TEST 1):

Any number can be increased by a percentage by converting the percentage into a decimal then adding 1 to that decimal and then multiplying the decimal by the number you want to increase by a percentage.

Step 1: Convert the percentage into a decimal by dividing the percentage by 100.

$$10\% = 10 \div 100 = 0.10$$

Step 2: Add 1 to the decimal

$$1 + 0.10 = 1.10$$

Step 3: Now multiply the cost of road tax in 2007 by 1.10 in order to find out what the new cost in 2008 for road tax is.

$$£120 \times 1.10 = £132$$

This means that road tax has increased in value by £12 and now costs £132 in 2008 rather than £120 as it did in 2007.

The answer to question 15 (Practice test 1) is **b.** £132

ANSWER TO QUESTION 16 (PRACTICE TEST 1)

Method 1

The price of one laptop is £850. If you wanted two of these laptops you would add £850 twice:

$$Price\ of\ 2\ laptops = £850 + £850$$

$$= £1,700$$

If you wanted 3 laptops, you would add £850 three times:

$$Price\ of\ 3\ laptops = £850 + 850 + £850$$

$$= £2,550$$

If you wanted 4 laptops, you would add £850 four times and so on. So if you wanted 12 laptops, priced at £850 each, you would need to add £850 twelve times.

Price of 12 laptops = £850 + £850 + £850 + £850 + £850 + £850

+ £850 + £850 + £850 + £850 + £850 + £850

= £10,200

12 laptops priced at £850 each would cost £10,200

Method 2

There is a quicker alternative to adding £850 twelve times. Simply multiply £850 by 12 which gives the same result as adding £850 together twelve times.

Price of 12 laptops = £850 × 12

= £10,200

The answer to question 16 (Practice test 1) is **a.** £10,200

ANSWER TO QUESTION 17 (PRACTICE TEST 1)

One metre of wool costs 62p. Buying 6 of these would equal:

Cost of 6 metres of wool = 62p × 6

= 372p

To convert any amount of pence into pound, divide the pence by 100 because 100 pence makes £1.

372p = 372 ÷ 100

= £3.72

Alternatively, you could add 62p six times to get the answer:

Cost of 6 metres of wool = 62p + 62p + 62p + 62p + 62p + 62p

= 372p

And *372p = £3.72*

The answer to question 17 (Practice test 1) is **a.** £3.72

ANSWER TO QUESTION 18 (PRACTICE TEST 1)

Firstly work out how many minutes Sally has to complete the course in. There are 60 minutes in 1 hour. This means that in 2 hours, there are:

$$60 \times 2 = 120 \text{ } minutes$$

In total Sally has been told that she has 2 hours and 30 minutes to complete the course. 2 hours represents 120 minutes, then simply add on 30 minutes to this:

$$2 \text{ } hours \text{ } 30 \text{ } minutes = 120 \text{ } minutes + 30 \text{ } minutes$$

$$= 150 \text{ minutes}$$

The next part of the question states: *"If divided into equal quarters, how long should she aim to spend completing each phase?"*.

A quarter means 'out of 4'. So to work out how long she should aim to spend completing each phase, divide the total minutes (150) by 4:

$$150 \div 4 = 37.5 \text{ } minutes$$

Sally should aim to complete each phase in 37.5 minutes.

The answer to question 18 is **b.** 37.5 minutes.

ANSWER TO QUESTION 19 (PRACTICE TEST 1)

18 teams need to share 6 changing rooms between them. To calculate how many teams use each changing room, divide the total number of teams by the number of changing rooms available to be used.

$$18 \div 6 = 3 \text{ } teams \text{ } in \text{ } each \text{ } changing \text{ } room$$

The answer to question 19 (Practice test 1) is **d.** 3

ANSWER TO QUESTION 20 (PRACTICE TEST 1)

A perimeter of an object is defined as the total length of all sides of the object. For the inner rectangle shown, both the longer sides are known. It's just the length of the dotted line at the bottom of the rectangle that we don't know.

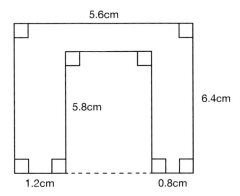

The top line of the outer, larger rectangle is 5.6 cm. This means that the entire bottom line must equal 5.6 cm. Two lengths on the bottom line are already given. To find the missing length, which is the dotted line, call x the length of the dotted line:

$$1.2cm + 0.8cm + x\ cm = 5.6cm$$

$$x\ cm = 5.6 - 1.2 - 0.8$$

$$= 3.6cm$$

The lengths of the inner rectangle are:

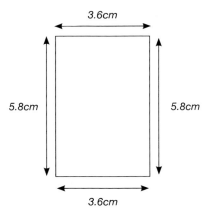

Adding the lengths of all sides of the rectangle will give the perimeter.

$$Perimeter = 3.6 + 3.6 + 5.8 + 5.8$$

$$= 18.8cm$$

The answer to question 20 (practice test 1) is **e. 18.8cm**

ANSWER TO QUESTION 21 (PRACTICE TEST 1)

Firstly calculate how many square metres the room measures by finding it's area. This can be achieved by multiplying the two measurements together.

$$Area\ of\ the\ room = 20m \times 5m = 100m^2$$

50% of anything is half of it, which means that 50% of 100m² would equal 50m². If you are not convinced, the calculation would be to convert 50% into a decimal and then multiply it by 100m²:

Step 1: Convert 50% into a decimal by dividing it by 100:

$$50\% = 50 \div 100$$

$$= 0.5$$

Step 2: Multiply 0.5 by 100m²

$$0.5 \times 100m^2 = 50m^2$$

If someone has 60m² of carpet but only needs to use 50m² of carpet then there would be:

$$60m^2 - 50m^2 = 10m^2\ of\ carpet\ left\ over.$$

The answer to question 21 (Practice test 1) is **b.** 10m2

ANSWER TO QUESTION 22 (PRACTICE TEST 1)

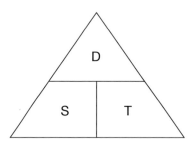

If you wanted a formula to calculate speed, simply place your thumb over S on the triangle. You will now see that $S = D/T$

The formula to use here is:

$$Speed\ (mph) = (distance\ (miles))/(time\ (hour)\ )$$

$$= 490 \text{ miles} \div 7 \text{ hours}$$

$$= 70 \text{ mph}$$

The answer to question 22 (Practice test 1) is **d.** 70 mph

ANSWER TO QUESTION 23 (PRACTICE TEST 1)

1 level at the car park contains 111 car parking spaces. This means that 8 levels will contain 8 times this amount.

$$\textit{Cars in the car park when it is full} = 8 \times 111$$

$$= 888 \textit{ cars}$$

The answer to question 23 (Practice test 1) is **b.** 888 cars

ANSWER TO QUESTION 24 (PRACTICE TEST 1)

The answer can be found by dividing the total win by how many employees there are. This will split the amount equally between all employees:

$$£1,500 \div 25 = £60$$

Each employee wins £60.

The answer to question 24 (Practice test 1) is **c.** £60

PRACTICE TEST 2

Q1. A yearly golf subscription costs £150 in 2012. It is expected to rise by 15% in 2013. How much will the yearly subscription cost in 2013?

    a. £172.50   **b.** £172.20   **c.** £172   **d.** £165.72   **e.** £162.50

Q2. In a cross country competition there are 138 runners, 23 runners do not finish the race. What is this as a fraction?

    a. 1/5   **b.** 1/6   **c.** 1/8   **d.** 1/12   **e.** 1/4

Q3. A football pitch is approximately 110 metres long. If you had 11 football pitches, one after the other, how long would the total distance be?

    a. 1,110 metres   **b.** 1,420 metres   **c.** 1,390 metres
    d. 1,440 metres   **e.** 1,210 metres

Q4. One out of twelve people in a group of football fans support Manchester United. If there are 2880 football fans, how many do not support Manchester United?

    a. 2420   **b.** 2640   **c.** 2680   **d.** 2740   **e.** 2520

Q5. A postman leaves the house at 08.00 hours and returns at 14.45 hours. How many hours has he been away from home?

    a. 5 hours 50 minutes   **b.** 5 hours 45 minutes   **c.** 6 hours 50 minutes
    d. 6 hours 45 minutes   **e.** 6 hours 15 minutes

Q6. You go to your local supermarket. You decide to buy some tomato soup. Each tin costs 14p. How much will 6 tins cost in total?

    a. 60p   **b.** 64p   **c.** 70p   **d.** 84p   **e.** 86p

Q7. One carpet tile measures 5cm by 5cm. How many tiles are required to cover a floor which measures 10m by 2m?

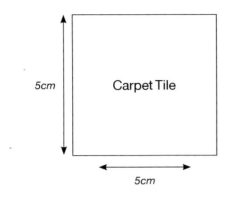

5cm

Carpet Tile

5cm

a. 705   **b.** 750   **c.** 8000   **d.** 8500   **e.** 9000

Q8. One power station supplies power to 34,000 homes. How many homes would 4 power stations supply?

a. 126,000   **b.** 128,000   **c.** 138,000   **d.** 148,000   **e.** 136,000

Q9. A drum contains 23 litres of oil. If a ship carries 11 drums of oil on-board, how many litres of oil are there altogether?

OIL

(23 litres)

a. 233 litres   **b.** 241 litres   **c.** 253 litres   **d.** 263 litres   **e.** 266 litres

Q10. A football match has an average of 32,000 spectators. There are 26 football matches a year. What is the total number of spectators throughout the year?

    a. 83,200   **b.** 832,000   **c.** 964,000   **d.** 110,600   **e.** 124,000

Q11. A library has 25 shelves of books. Each shelf holds 700 books. How many books are in the library?

    a. 1,750   **b.** 17,050   **c.** 17,500   **d.** 35,000   **e.** 38,500

Q12. At an allotment there are 3 plots: plot A, plot B and plot C. Using the diagram below, calculate the area of plot B.

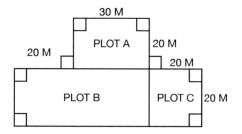

    a. 1,000 m²   **b.** 2,500 m²   **c.** 2,000 m²   **d.** 3,000 m²   **e.** 100 m²

Q13. What is the average value of the following: 14, 28, 47, 47, 60 and 104?

    a. 50   **b.** 53   **c.** 55   **d.** 60   **e.** 62

Q14. There are 44 police forces in the United Kingdom. Each police force has 14 Senior Officers. How many Senior Officers are there in total?

    a. 561   **b.** 606   **c.** 616   **d.** 861   **e.** 882

Q15. A company has to dismiss 1 out of 6 of their employees. If the company employs 636 people, how many will the company have to dismiss?

    a. 96   **b.** 103   **c.** 106   **d.** 126   **e.** 132

Q16. If 6 out of 24 employees become managers, what is this as a fraction?

    a. 1/4   **b.** 2/4   **c.** 1/8   **d.** 1/6   **e.** 1/3

Q17. You go to the local shop and buy a magazine costing £2.40 and a drink costing £1.12. How much change do you get from a £10 note?

    a. £6.52   **b.** £4.48   **c.** £5.52   **d.** £6.48   **e.** £6.56

Q18. A cruise ship can carry 90,000 passengers. On this occasion the ship is only 75% full. How many passengers are on board?

    a. 6,750   **b.** 13,500   **c.** 54,500   **d.** 67,500   **e.** 68,250

Q19. A car garage sells 50 cars per month. 2 % of these are returned with engine problems. How many cars with engine problems are returned to the car garage each year?

    a. 6   **b.** 9   **c.** 13   **d.** 15   **e.** 12

Q20. A Formula 1 car drives 660 miles in 3 hours 40 minutes. What is its average speed?

    a. 160 mph   **b.** 190 mph   **c.** 180 mph   **d.** 185 mph   **e.** 190 mph

Q21. You can run 2 miles in 18 minutes. How long does it take you to run 0.5 miles at this speed?

    a. 4 minutes 30 seconds   **b.** 5 minutes   **c.** 6 minute 30 seconds
    d. 4 minutes 20 seconds   **e.** 5 minutes 10 seconds

Q22. You walk to school and it takes you 20 minutes. You know that you walk an average of 3 mph. How far is school from your house?

    a. 2 miles   **b.** 1 mile   **c.** 6 miles   **d.** 4 miles   **e.** 5 miles

Q23. A farmer has 650 sheep. He keeps his sheep in 5 large fields. How many sheep does he have in each field?

    a. 120   **b.** 130   **c.** 150   **d.** 160   **e.** 170

Q24. A delivery driver has to drive on average 12,000 miles a month. If the driver works every day in April, how many miles does he have to drive each day?

    a. 200 miles   **b.** 300 miles   **c.** 350 miles   **d.** 387 miles   **e.** 400 miles

Q25. You withdraw 30% of your savings from an account which holds £600. How much remains in the account?

    a. £360   **b.** £390   **c.** £420   **d.** £430   **e.** £45

ANSWERS TO PRACTICE TEST 2

ANSWER TO QUESTION 1 (PRACTICE TEST 2)

Any number can be increased by a percentage by converting the percentage into a decimal then adding 1 to that decimal and then multiplying the decimal by the number you want to increase by a percentage.

Step 1: Convert the percentage into a decimal by dividing the percentage by 100.

$$15\% = 15 \div 100 = 0.15$$

Step 2: Add 1 to the decimal

$$1 + 0.15 = 1.15$$

Step 3: Now multiply the cost of a yearly golf subscription in 2012 by 1.15 in order to increase it by 15% and find out what the new cost in 2013 is for a yearly subscription.

$$£150 \times 1.15 = £172.50$$

This means that a yearly golf subscription has increased in value by £22.50 and will now costs £172.50 in 2013 rather than £150 as it did in 2012.

The answer to question 1 (Practice test 2) is **a)** £172.50

ANSWER TO QUESTION 2 (PRACTICE TEST 2)

23 out of 138 runners do not finish the race. This can be written in fraction form as:

$$\frac{23}{138}$$

23 goes into 138 six times. The fraction can now be written as:

$$\frac{23}{138} = \frac{1}{6}$$

The answer to question 2 (Practice test 2) is **b.** 1/6

ANSWER TO QUESTION 3 (PRACTICE TEST 2)

If one football pitch is 110 metres long, two football pitches will be 110 + 110 = 220 metres long, three football pitches will be 110 + 110 + 110 = 330 metres long and so on.

A quick way to find out how long 11 football pitches would be is to multiply the length of one pitch by 11.

$$Length\ of\ 11\ football\ pitches = 11 \times 110$$

$$= 1,210\ metres$$

The answer to question 3 (Practice test 3) is   **e.** 1,210 metres.

ANSWER TO QUESTION 4 (PRACTICE TEST 2)

Method 1

1 out of every 12 fans support Manchester United and there are 2880 football fans. To calculate how many fans support Manchester United:

$$\frac{1}{12} \times 2880 = 2880 \div 12$$

$$= 240\ fans\ support\ Manchester\ United$$

If 240 out of the 2880 fans support Manchester United, this means that:

$$2880 - 240 = 2640\ fans\ DO\ NOT\ support\ Manchester\ United$$

Method 2

1 out of every 12 fans support Manchester United which means that 11 out of 12 fans DO NOT support Manchester united.

$$\frac{11}{12} \times 2880 = 2640$$

The answer to question 4 (Practice test 2) is **b.** 2640

ANSWER TO QUESTION 5 (PRACTICE TEST 2)

From 8 am to 2 pm is 6 hours. Add the 45 minutes to this to get 6 hours 45 minutes.

The answer to question 5 (Practice test 2) is **d.** 6 hours 45 minutes

ANSWER TO QUESTION 6 (PRACTICE TEST 2)

$$Cost\ of\ 6\ tins = 14p \times 6$$

$$= 84p$$

The answer to question 6 (Practice test 2) is **d.** 84p

ANSWER TO QUESTION 7 (PRACTICE TEST 2)

Note: The carpet tile measurement is given in centimetres (cm) and the floor measurement is given in metres (m). Only one common unit can be used so either convert centimetres into metres or vice versa before proceeding with any calculations. Use the following conversion to convert metres into cm's:

$$1\ m = 100\ cm$$

Using centimetres (cm):

The floor measures 10m by 2m. In cm's:

$10m = 10 \times 100 = 1000cm$

$2m = 2 \times 100 = 200cm$

Area of the floor = 1000cm × 200cm = **200,000cm²**

The area one carpet tile measures = 5cm × 5cm = **25cm²**

To find how many tiles with a 25cm² area will cover a floor 200,000cm² in area, simply divide the area of the floor by the area of one tile.

Number of tiles required to cover a floor 200,000cm² in area:

$$200000\ cm^2 \div 25cm^2 = 8000\ tiles$$

Using metres (m)

$5cm = 5 \div 100 = 0.05m$

*The area one carpet tile measures = 0.05m × 0.05m = **0.0025m²***

*Area of the floor = 10m × 2m = **20m²***

Number of tiles required to cover a floor 20m² in area:

20m² ÷ 0.0025m² = 8000 tiles

The answer to question 7 (practice test 2) is **c.** 8000

ANSWER TO QUESTION 8 (PRACTICE TEST 2)

If one power station supplies power to 34,000 homes, then 4 power stations would supply 4 times the amount of homes that one power station supplies:

Four power stations supplies: 34,000 × 4 = 136,000 *homes*

The answer to question 8 (practice test 2) is   **e.** 136,000

ANSWER TO QUESTION 9 (PRACTICE TEST 2)

One drum contains 23 litres of oil; therefore 11 drums would carry 11 times the amount one drum contains.

Total litres of oil on the ship = Amount of oil one drum contains × 11

= 23 litres × 11

= 253 litres

The answer to question 9 (Practice test 2) is **c.** 253 litres

ANSWER TO QUESTION 10 (PRACTICE TEST 2)

One match has 32,000 spectators, so 26 matches will have 26 times the number of spectators:

32,000 × 26 = 832,000 spectators

The answer to question 10 (Practice test 2) is **b.** 832,000

ANSWER TO QUESTION 11 (PRACTICE TEST 2)

$$700 \times 25 = 17,500$$

The answer to question 11 (Practice Test 2) is **c.** 17,500

ANSWER TO QUESTION 12 (PRACTICE TEST 2)

The horizontal edge of plot B is 20m + 30m = 50m

The vertical edge is 20m (same as the plot C).

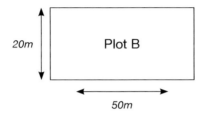

To calculate the area multiply the length and width of plot B:

$$Area\ of\ plot\ B = 50 \times 20 = 1000m^2$$

The answer to question12 (Practice Test 2) is **a.** $1000m^2$

ANSWER TO QUESTION 13 (PRACTICE TEST 2)

To calculate the average, add all the numbers together and divide by how many numbers there are:

$$Average = \frac{14 + 28 + 47 + 47 + 60 + 104}{6} = \frac{300}{6} = 50$$

The answer to question 13 (Practice Test 2) is **a.** 50

ANSWER TO QUESTION 14 (PRACTICE TEST 2)

$$44 \times 14 = 616\ \textit{senior officers in total}$$

The answer to question 14 (Practice test 2) is **c.** 616

ANSWER TO QUESTION 15 (PRACTICE TEST 2)

1 out of every 6 employees will be dismissed. As a fraction this is:

$$\frac{1}{6}$$

If 636 people are employed the calculation to find the amount of employees dismissed is:

$$636 \times \frac{1}{6} = 106 \; employees$$

The answer to question 15 (Practice Test 2) is **c.** 106 employees.

ANSWER TO QUESTION 16 (PRACTICE TEST 2)

$$\frac{6}{24}$$

This can be reduced by dividing both the top and bottom numbers of the fraction by 6.

$$\frac{6}{24} = \frac{1}{4}$$

The answer to question 16 (Practice Test 2) is **a.** 1/4

ANSWER TO QUESTION 17 (PRACTICE TEST 2)

$$£10 – £2.40 – £1.12 = £6.48$$

The answer to question 17 (Practice Test 2) is £6.48

ANSWER TO QUESTION 18 (PRACTICE TEST 2)

75% means 75 out of a 100. As a fraction this can be written as $\frac{75}{100}$

As a decimal this is 0.75.

To find how many passengers are on board multiply 90,000 by the decimal or fraction.

Using the decimal:

$$0.75 \times 90{,}000 = 67{,}500 \; passengers$$

Using the fraction:

$$\frac{75}{100} \times 90{,}000 = 67{,}500 \; passengers$$

The answer to question 18 (Practice Test 2) is **d.** 67,500

ANSWER TO QUESTION 19 (PRACTICE TEST 2)

75% means 75 out of a 100. As a fraction this can be written as $\dfrac{2}{100}$

As a decimal this is 0.02.

To find how many cars are returned with engine problems per month, multiply 50 by the decimal or fraction.

Using the decimal:

$$0.02 \times 50 = 1 \; car$$

Using the fraction:

$$\frac{2}{100} \times 50 = 1 \; car$$

1 car is returned per month. As there are 12 months in a year, 12 cars are returned over 1 year.

The answer to question 19 (Practice Test 2) is **e.** 12

ANSWER TO QUESTION 20 (PRACTICE TEST 2)

$$Speed = \frac{distance}{time}$$

Time needs to be in hours before it can be inserted into the above formula. 3 hours is fine. But 40 minutes needs to be in terms of hours.

To convert minutes into hours divide by 60.

$$40 \; minutes = \frac{40}{60} = 0.66666...hours$$

Therefore, 3 hours 40 minutes is 3.666666....hours.

$$Speed = \frac{660}{3.66666} = 180mph$$

The answer to question 20 (Practice Test 2) is **c.** 180mph

ANSWER TO QUESTION 21 (PRACTICE TEST 2)

2 miles were covered in 18 minutes. Therefore, 1 mile would be covered in 9 minutes. Half this again and therefore, 0.5 miles would be covered in 4.5 minutes i.e. 4 and a half minutes. This is the same as 4 minutes 30 seconds as 30 seconds is half a minute.

The answer to question 21 (Practice Test 2) is **a.** 4 minutes 30 seconds

ANSWER TO QUESTION 22 (PRACTICE TEST 2)

$$20 \; minutes \; in \; hours = 20 \div 60 = 0.333333...hours$$

$$Distance = speed \times time$$

$$= 3 \times 0.333333$$

$$= 1 \; mile$$

The answer to question 22 (Practice Test 2) is **b.** 1 mile

ANSWER TO QUESTION 23 (PRACTICE TEST 2)

$$\frac{650}{5} = 130 \; sheep \; in \; each \; field$$

The answer to question 23 (Practice Test 2) is **b.** 130

ANSWER TO QUESTION 24 (PRACTICE TEST 2)

There are 30 days in April. If he drives 12,000 miles for 30 days (1 month) then for 1 day he drives:

$$\frac{12{,}000}{30} = 400 \; miles$$

The answer to question 24 (Practice Test 2) is **e.** 400 miles

ANSWER TO QUESTION 25 (PRACTICE TEST 2)

If 30% is withdrawn from the account this means that 70% still remains. 70% means 70 out of a 100. As a fraction this can be written as 70/100

As a decimal this is 0.70

To find how much remains in the account, multiply 600 by the decimal or fraction.

Using the decimal:

$$0.70 \times 600 = £420$$

Using the fraction:

$$\frac{70}{100} \times 600 = £420$$

This means that £420 remains in the account after 30% is withdrawn.

The answer to question 25 (Practice Test 2) is **c.** £420

PRACTICE TEST 3

Q1. In the Johnson family there are 7 people; 3 of them are female. What is this as a fraction?

    a. 2/3   **b.** 4/6   **c.** 3/7   **d.** 6/15   **e.** 1/3

Q2. You are at a traffic collision where a vehicle has crashed into a play area.

As part of your documentation you need to calculate the area of the playing field. Use the diagram below to work out the area of the playing field.

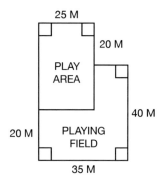

    a. 700 m²   **b.** 900 m²   **c.** 1,200 m²   **d.** 1,300 m²   **e.** 1,400 m²

Q3. Your yearly salary is £40,000. You also receive a yearly bonus which is 15% of your salary. How much do you earn per year?

    a. £40,060   **b.** £40,600   **c.** £46,000   **d.** £49,000   **e.** £56,000

Q4. On a housing estate there are 34,000 homes. Of these homes 63% are semi-detached, 30% are detached, and the remainder are terraced houses. How many houses are terraced?

    a. 23.8   **b.** 238   **c.** 2,380   **d.** 2,680   **e.** 23,800

Q5. An Army soldier has two foot patrols a day. The total distance walked is 20 miles. If the soldier walked an average speed of 4 mph, how long is each patrol?

    a. 5 hours   **b.** 3 hours 30 minutes   **c.** 4 hours
    d. 2 hours 30 minutes   **e.** 4 hours 20 minutes

Q6. You are tasked to drive your boss to a meeting 100 miles away. You will be driving at 60 mph. If you set off at 10:20pm, what time would you arrive?

    a. 11:40pm   **b.** 12:00pm   **c.** 12:40pm   **d.** 12:20pm   **e.** 12:30pm

Q7. A criminal sprints at a speed of 10 metres every 2 seconds (10m / 2 seconds). How long does it take him to run 1,000 metres if he continues at the same speed?

    a. 100 seconds   **b.** 10 seconds   **c.** 200 seconds
    d. 20 seconds   **e.** 25 seconds

Q8. You are at a fruit and vegetable stall at a market. If one apple costs 41p, how much would it cost to buy 11 apples?

    a. £4.41   **b.** £4.21   **c.** £4.61   **d.** £4.67   **e.** £4.51

Q9. A car garage orders four new sport cars costing £41,000 each. How much in total has the garage spent on the new sports cars?

    a. £124,000   **b.** £154,000   **c.** £164,000
    d. £166,000   **e.** £168,000

Q10. A water tank has a maximum capacity of 200 litres. If the tank is 80% full how many more litres are required to fill it to its maximum?

    a. 25 litres   **b.** 40 litres   **c.** 50 litres   **d.** 55 litres   **e.** 60 litres

Q11. If I spend £1.60, £2.35, £3.55 and £4.75 on a selection of goods, how much will I have spent in total?

    a. £10.65   **b.** £11.60   **c.** £11.55   **d.** £12.25   **e.** £12.55

Q12. On Monday it takes Lucy 52 minutes to get to work. On Tuesday it takes 40 minutes, Wednesday takes 51 minutes, on Thursday it takes 1 hour 2 minutes and on Friday it takes 1 hour 30 minutes. How long did her average commute take?

    a. 58 minutes   **b.** 62 minutes   **c.** 60 minutes
    d. 61 minutes   **e.** 59 minutes

Q13. Paul is a 100 metre sprinter. During a weekend-long competition he runs the distance in 11 seconds, 9 seconds, 9.5 seconds and 11.5 seconds. What is the average time that Paul runs 100 metres in?

    a. 9 seconds   **b.** 10 second   **c.** 11 seconds
    d. 10.25 seconds   **e.** 10.5 seconds

Q14. One in fourteen people become a victim of car crime each year. In Saxby there are 224 people. On that basis, how many people per year experience car crime in Saxby?

    a. 14   **b.** 16   **c.** 18   **d.** 20   **e.** 22

Q15. Lisa's weekly newspaper bill is £5.50 and the delivery charge is 35p per week. How much does she have to pay over six weeks?

    a. £28.10   **b.** £31.10   **c.** £35.10   **d.** £35.20   **e.** £36.10

Q16. A gardener wants to gravel over the area shown below. One bag of gravel will cover 20m². How many bags are needed to cover the entire garden?

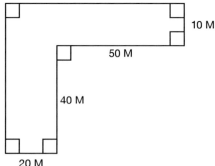

    a. 40   **b.** 55   **c.** 65   **d.** 75   **e.** 130

Q17. The gardener decides he is only going to gravel 20% of the garden. Using the above diagram, how many square metres will he be gravelling?

    a. 26 m²   **b.** 300 m²   **c.** 130 m²   **d.** 240 m²   **e.** 260 m²

Q18. You are a Police officer and you stop and search 40 people. 8 of them are arrested for possession of a class 'A' drug. What is this as a fraction?

    a. 1/3   **b.** 1/4   **c.** 1/6   **d.** 1/10   **e.** 1/5

Q19. There are 144 people entered into a raffle, 12 people each win a prize. What is this as a fraction?

    a. 1/6   **b.** 1/8   **c.** 1/12   **d.** 1/24   **e.** 1/10

Q20. At a music festival there are 35,000 festival goers, 5% of these are under 16 years of age. How many festival goers were under 16?

    a. 1500   **b.** 1750   **c.** 2500   **d.** 3500   **e.** 7000

Q21. At Christmas you buy 30 presents; 12 are bought for your family and 18 for your friends. What percentage was bought for your friends?

    a. 20%   **b.** 30%   **c.** 40%   **d.** 60%   **e.** 75%

Q22. Over one year, PC Smith files details of 600 drink driving cases. These are divided into 5 piles dependent upon how over the limit the drink driver was. If the piles are all equal sizes, how many are in each pile?

    a. 115 files   **b.** 120 files   **c.** 125 files   **d.** 130 files   **e.** 135 files

Q23. On average, 1 out of every 30 people experience back problems in their lifetime. Out of 900 people, how many will experience back problems?

    a. 20   **b.** 30   **c.** 60   **d.** 90   **e.** 120

ANSWERS TO PRACTICE TEST 3

ANSWER TO QUESTION 1 (PRACTICE TEST 3)

3 out of a total of 7 are female. This can be written as 3/7

The answer to question 1 (Practice Test 3) is **c.** 3/7

ANSWER TO QUESTION 2 (PRACTICE TEST 3)

The area of any rectangle or square shape can be found by multiplying two of the lengths together. In this case, the playing field has a length of 40m vertically and a length of 35m horizontally. Multiplying the two of these will give the area of the playing field:

$$Area\ of\ playing\ field = 35m \times 40m$$

$$= 1400m^2$$

Don't forget, area is always squared. In this case, the answer is 1400 metres squared. Regardless of which unit is used i.e. centimetres, millimetres, inches etc an area must always be squared.

The answer to question 2 (Practice Test 3) is **e.** 1,400 m^2

ANSWER TO QUESTION 3 (PRACTICE TEST 3)

Calculate the value of the yearly bonus by working out what 15% of £40,000 is.

15% can be written as a decimal by dividing it by 100 to give 0.15.

To find 15% of £40,000 multiply 0.15 by £40,000.

0.15 × £40,000 = £6000

Therefore, the yearly bonus is £6,000. On top of a salary of £40,000 this makes the total earnings per year £40,000 + £6,000 = £46,000

The answer to question 3 (Practice Test 3) is **c.** £46,000

ANSWER TO QUESTION 4 (PRACTICE TEST 3)

Semi-detached homes (63%)
63% as a decimal is 0.63. Multiplying this by 34,000 homes will give the number of semi-detached homes on the housing estate:

$$0.63 \times 34{,}000 = 21{,}420 \text{ semi-detached homes}$$

Detached homes (30%)
30% as a decimal is 0.30. Multiplying this by 34,000 homes will give the number of detached homes on the housing estate:

$$0.30 \times 34{,}000 = 10{,}200 \text{ detached homes}$$

Terraced homes
The total number of homes, 34,000 includes all the semi-detached, detached and terraced homes added together. To find the number of terraced homes only, subtract the number of semi-detached and detached homes from the total number of homes, which will then leave the number of terraced homes.

$$\text{Number of terraced homes} = 34{,}000 - 21{,}420 - 10{,}200$$

$$= 2{,}380 \text{ homes}$$

The answer to question 4 (Practice Test 3) is **c.** 2,380 terraced homes.

ANSWER TO QUESTION 5 (PRACTICE TEST 3)

$$Time = \frac{distance}{speed}$$

The distance is 20 miles and the speed is 4 miles per hour. Both of these are in the correct units. Note that because the speed is in 'miles per hour' when a value for 'time' is calculated this will be time in hours.

$$Time = \frac{20 \text{ miles}}{4 \text{ mph}}$$

$$= 5 \text{ hours}$$

The answer to question 5 (Practice Test 3) is **a.** 5 hours

ANSWER TO QUESTION 6 (PRACTICE TEST 3)

$$Time = \frac{distance}{speed}$$

The distance is 100 miles and the speed is 60 miles per hour. Both of these are in the units required to calculate time in hours. Note that because the distance is in miles and speed is in 'miles per hour' when a value for 'time' is calculated this will be time in hours.

$$Time = \frac{100\ miles}{60\ mph}$$

$$= 1.666666667 \text{ hours}$$

1. 666666667 hours is the same as 1 hour and 40 minutes. It is important to not confuse '0.666666667' hours as being '0.666666667' minutes. To convert 0.666666667 hours into minutes, multiply it by 60.

0.666666667 hours in minutes = 0.666666667 × 60 = **40 minutes**

This means it took 1 hour and 40 minutes. If you set off at 10.20pm you would arrive 1 hour and 40 minutes later, which would make it midnight, 12.00pm

The answer to question 6 (Practice Test 3) is **b.** 12:00pm

ANSWER TO QUESTION 7 (PRACTICE TEST 3)

10 metres are covered every 2 seconds. 1,000 metres is 100 times greater than 10 metres. Therefore, multiply 2 seconds by 100 to find the amount of time it takes to run 1,000 metres.

$$Time\ take\ to\ run\ 1,000\ metres = 2 \times 100$$

$$= 200 \text{ seconds}$$

The answer to question 7 (Practice Test 3) is **c.** 200 seconds

ANSWER TO QUESTION 8 (PRACTICE TEST 3)

One apple costs 41p so 11 apples would cost 11 multiplied by 41p.

$$Cost\ of\ 11\ apples = 11 \times 41p = 451p$$

To convert pence into pounds, divide the pence by 100 as there are 100 pence in a pound.

$$451p \ in \ pounds = £4.51$$

Therefore, it would cost £4.51 to buy 11 apples.

The answer to question 8 (Practice Test 3) is **e.** £4.51

ANSWER TO QUESTION 9 (PRACTICE TEST 3)

$$£41,000 \times 4 = £164,000$$

The answer to question 9 (Practice Test 3) is **c.** £164,000

ANSWER TO QUESTION 10 (PRACTICE TEST 3)

$$80\% \ as \ a \ decimal = 0.8$$

To calculate 80% of 200 litres, which will give the amount of litres in the tank when it is 80% full, multiply 0.8 by 200 litres (the maximum capacity):

$$Litres \ in \ the \ tank \ when \ 80\% \ full = 0.8 \times 200 = 160 \ litres$$

If the tank has a maximum capacity of 200 litres, then there are 40 more litres required to fill it to its maximum if the tank is 160 litres full. This can be found by subtracting the maximum capacity of the tank by the amount already in the tank:

$$Amount \ of \ litres \ required \ to \ fill \ the \ tank = 200 - 160 = 40 \ litres$$

The answer to question 10 (Practice Test 3) is **b.** 40 litres

ANSWER TO QUESTION 11 (PRACTICE TEST 3)

$$Total \ amount \ spent = £1.60 + £2.35 + £3.55 + £4.75$$

$$= £12.25$$

The answer to question 11 (Practice Test 3) is **d.** £12.25

ANSWER TO QUESTION 12 (PRACTICE TEST 3)

To calculate the average, add all the times together and then divide by how many days. Remember that 1 hour is 60 minutes.

Monday: 52 minutes

Tuesday: 40 minutes

Wednesday: 51 minutes

Thursday: 1 hour 2 minutes = 62 mins

Friday: 1 hour 30 minutes = 90 minutes

$$Total\ time = 52 + 40 + 51 + 62 + 90 = 295\ minutes$$

Now divide this by the total amount of days which is 5.

$$Average\ commute = 295 \div 5 = 59\ minutes$$

The answer to question 12 (Practice Test 3) is **e.** 59 *minutes*

ANSWER TO QUESTION 13 (PRACTICE TEST 3)

To find the average, find the sum of all the times by adding them together and then divide by how many times there are.

$$Average = \frac{11 + 9 + 9.5 + 11.5}{4}$$

$$= \frac{41}{4}$$

$$= 10.25\ seconds$$

The answer to question 13 (Practice Test 3) is **d.** 10.25 seconds

ANSWER TO QUESTION 14 (PRACTICE TEST 3)

1 person of out 14 is a victim of car crime per year. If there are 224 people, divide this by 14 to find how many people per year are a victim of car crime.

$$Victims\ of\ car\ crime\ per\ year\ in\ Saxby = 224 \div 14$$

$$= 16\ victims\ per\ year$$

The answer to question 14 (Practice Test 3) is **b.** 16

ANSWER TO QUESTION 15 (PRACTICE TEST 3)

35p in pounds is £0.35

$$Total\ charge\ per\ week = £5.50 + £0.35 = £5.85$$

For six weeks, multiply the cost per week by 6

$$Total\ charge\ for\ six\ weeks = £5.85 \times 6$$

$$= £35.10$$

The answer to question 15 (Practice Test 3) is **c.** £35.10

ANSWER TO QUESTION 16 (PRACTICE TEST 3)

It is necessary to calculate the entire area of the garden in order to find how many bags of gravel are required to cover it.

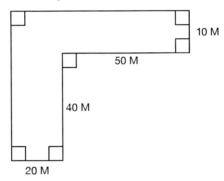

$$Area\ of\ the\ top\ horizontal\ rectangle = 10m \times 70m = 700m^2$$

$$Area\ of\ vertical\ rectangle = 40m \times 20m = 800m^2$$

$$Total\ area\ of\ the\ garden = 700m^2 + 800m^2$$

$$= 1500m^2$$

One bag of gravel covers $20m^2$. To calculate how many bags of gravel are required to cover $1500m^2$ use the following calculation:

$$Amount\ of\ gravel\ bags\ required = 1500m^2 \div 20m^2$$

$$= 75\ bags$$

The answer to question 16 (Practice Test 3) is **d.** 75 bags

ANSWER TO QUESTION 17 (PRACTICE TEST 3)

Using the total area of the garden from question 16:

$$Total\ area\ of\ the\ garden = 700m^2 + 800m^2$$

$$= 1500m^2$$

$20\%\ as\ a\ decimal = 20 \div 100$

$$= 0.2$$

$20\%\ of\ 1500 = 0.2 \times 1,500m^2$

$$= 300m^2$$

The gardener will be gravelling $300m^2$

The answer to question 17 (Practice Test 3) is **b.** $300m^2$

ANSWER TO QUESTION 18 (PRACTICE TEST 3)

As a fraction this is 8/40 which can be simplified further by dividing the top and bottom of the fraction by 8.

$8 \div 8 = 1$ and

$40 \div 8 = 5$

Therefore, $\dfrac{8}{40} = \dfrac{1}{5}$

The answer to question 19 (Practice Test 3) is **e.** 1/5

ANSWER TO QUESTION 19 (PRACTICE TEST 3)

12 out of 144 people win a prize. As a fraction this can be written as:

$$\frac{12}{144}$$

Both the top and bottom of the fraction can then be divided by 12 to simplify the fraction which leaves:

$$\frac{12}{144} = \frac{1}{12}$$

The answer to question 19 (Practice Test 3) is **c.** 1/12

ANSWER TO QUESTION 20 (PRACTICE TEST 3)

$$5\% \text{ as a decimal} = \frac{5}{100} = 0.05$$

To find what 5% of 35,000 is, multiply 0.05 by 35,000. This will give the number of festival goers that were under 16.

$$\text{Number of festival goers under } 16 = 0.05 \times 35,000$$

$$= 1,750$$

The answer to question 20 (Practice Test 3) is **b.** 1,750

ANSWER TO QUESTION 21 (PRACTICE TEST 3)

As a fraction, 18 out of 30 (18/30) presents were bought for friends. To convert fractions into a percentage multiply the fraction by 100.

$$\frac{18}{30} \times 100 = 60\%$$

The answer to question 21 (Practice Test 3) is **d.** 60%

ANSWER TO QUESTION 22 (PRACTICE TEST 3)

$$600 \div 5 = 120 \text{ piles}$$

The answer to question 22 (Practice Test 3) is **b.** 120 files

ANSWER TO QUESTION 23 (PRACTICE TEST 3)

For every 30 people, 1 person will experience a back problem. If there are 900 people:

$$900 \div 30 = 30 \text{ people will experience back problems}$$

The answer to question 23 (Practice Test 3) is **b.** 30

PRACTICE TEST 4

Q1. Billy can run 1.5 miles in 12 minutes. How long does it take him to run 12 miles if he continues at the same speed?

    a. 1 hour 26 minutes   **b.** 1 hour 12 minutes   **c.** 1 hour 36 minutes
    d. 1 hour 6 minutes   **e.** 1 hour 20 minutes

Q2. Jennifer runs 39 miles in 4 hours 20 minutes. What was her average speed?

    a. 12 mph   **b.** 10 mph   **c.** 9 mph   **d.** 7 mph   **e.** 8 mph

Q3. A helicopter flies a distance of 840 miles in 6 hours. What speed is it flying at in miles per hour?

    a. 140 mph   **b.** 160 mph   **c.** 150 mph   **d.** 145 mph   **e.** 135 mph

Q4. Emma works 5 days a week. Every day she drives 20 miles to work, and 20 miles back. She drives at an average speed of 30 mph. How much time does Emma spend driving to work and back each working week?

    a. 6 hours 40 minutes   **b.** 6 hours 15 minutes   **c.** 6 hours 20 minutes
    d. 6 hours 45 minutes   **e.** 7 hours

Q5. You are driving to a meeting at 96 mph. The meeting is 24 miles away.

How long will it take you to get to the meeting?

    a. 12 minutes   **b.** 15 minutes   **c.** 10 minutes
    d. 20 minutes   **e.** 25 minutes

Q6. You are driving at 42 mph for 20 minutes. How far have you come?

    a. 14 miles   **b.** 20 miles   **c.** 17 miles   **d.** 15 miles   **e.** 16 miles

Q7. In a year 20,600 people are arrested. One quarter of these is over 50 years of age. How many people over 50 years of age are arrested?

    a. 4,150   **b.** 4,300   **c.** 5,350   **d.** 5,200   **e.** 5,150

Q8. If 2 out of 10 entrants won at a dog show, how many would win if there were 100 entrants at the show?

    a. 10   **b.** 15   **c.** 20   **d.** 35   **e.** 40

Q9. Calculate the perimeter of the shape below.

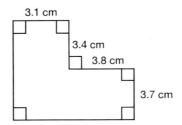

    a. 18.4 cm   **b.** 28.0 cm   **c.** 28.4 cm   **d.** 32.0 cm   **e.** 32.8 cm

Q10. An office has a floor space of 21,000 m_c. If 700 people work in the office, how much m_c space does each employee have?

    a. 3 m_c **b.** 30 m_c **c.** 60 m_c **d.** 90 m_c **e.** 300 m_c

Q11. New Army boots cost £112; you are subsidised £42 from the service to contribute towards the boots. How much will you need to contribute?

    a. £60   **b.** £62   **c.** £58   **d.** £74   **e.** £70

Q12. I have £13 in my wallet and spend £4.37 shopping. How much do I have left?

    a. £8.73   **b.** £7.63   **c.** £8.63   **d.** £6.85   **e.** £6.53

Q13. How much do 24 boxes of chocolates cost at £4.10 each?

    a. £98.20   **b.** £78.20   **c.** £88.40   **d.** £94.40   **e.** £98.40

Q14. Police in Horncastle pull over 200 suspected drink drivers over a 6 month period. There are 36 people over the drink driving limit. Out of the 200, what percentage are over the legal limit?

    a. 16%   **b.** 18%   **c.** 24%   **d.** 30%   **e.** 36%

Q15. Each year 15,000 Paramedics are recruited in Scotland. 30% are female.

How many male Paramedics are recruited in Scotland each year?

    a. 4500   **b.** 7500   **c.** 10500   **d.** 12500   **e.** 15000

Q16. What is the average age of a group of children whose individual ages are: 11 years, 13 years, 9 years, 9 years, and 8 years?

    a. 10 years   **b.** 11 years   **c.** 12 years   **d.** 13 years   **e.** 14 years

Q17. How much would it cost to buy 26 jars of jam at £1.15 per jar?

    a. £26.90   **b.** £27.60   **c.** £28.50   **d.** £29.45   **e.** £29.90

Q18. There are 635 boxes in a lorry. How many boxes would there be in 3 lorries?

    a. 1,605   **b.** 1,805   **c.** 1,850   **d.** 1,905   **e.** 1,980

Q19. In a pick and mix you get 25 sweets in a bag for £4.00. How much does each sweet cost?

    a. £0.10   **b.** £0.16   **c.** £1.00   **d.** £1.60   **e.** £1.80

Q20. Whilst hiking you walk a total distance of 725 miles over a 5-day period.

On average, how many miles did you walk a day?

    a. 145 miles   **b.** 150 miles   **c.** 125 miles   **d.** 90 miles   **e.** 160 miles

Q21. A crime investigator is carrying out research into the market value of narcotics. He is given four values for an eighth of an ounce of cannabis: £19, £22, £21.75, and £25.25. What is the average value for an eighth of an ounce of cannabis?

    a. £17   **b.** £19   **c.** £21   **d.** £22   **e.** £24

Q22. Your business has yearly profits of £520,000. There are 13 equal share holders in the company. How much does each individual make in profit?

    a. £20,000   **b.** £30,000   **c.** £35,000   **d.** £40,000   **e.** £42,000

ANSWERS TO PRACTICE TEST 4

ANSWER TO QUESTION 1 (PRACTICE TEST 4)

The question gives a distance and time from which Billy's speed can be calculated using the equation below.

$$Speed = \frac{distance}{time}$$

Billy runs 1.5 miles in 12 minutes. The time needs to be in hours. To convert minutes into hours divide the minutes by 60:

$$12\ minutes\ in\ hours = \frac{12}{60} = 0.2\ hours$$

Now the speed can be calculated:

$$Speed = \frac{1.5\ miles}{0.2\ hours} = 7.5\ mph$$

Now that Billy's speed is known, the time it would take Billy to cover 12 miles can be found using the following formula:

$$Time = \frac{distance}{speed} = \frac{12}{7.5} = 1.6\ hours$$

1.6 does not mean 1 hour 6 minutes. To convert 0.6 hours into minutes, multiply 0.6 by 60:

$$0.6\ hours\ in\ minutes = 36\ minutes$$

The total time it would take Billy to cover 12 miles would be 1 hour 36 minutes.

The answer to question 1 (Practice Test 4) is **c.** 1 hour 36 minutes

ANSWER TO QUESTION 2 (PRACTICE TEST 4)

Using the speed formula, the time needs to in hours. To convert 20 minutes into hours divide by 60:

$$20 \text{ minutes in hours} = 20/60$$

$$= 0.33333 \text{ recurring}$$

$$4 \text{ hours } 20 \text{ minutes} = 4.333333.... \text{ hours}$$

$$Speed = \frac{distance}{time}$$

$$Speed = \frac{39}{4.33333....} = 9 \text{ mph}$$

The answer to question 2 (Practice Test 4) is **c.** 9 mph

ANSWER TO QUESTION 3 (PRACTICE TEST 4)

$$Speed = \frac{840 \text{ miles}}{6 \text{ hours}} = 140 \text{ mph}$$

The answer to question 3 (Practice Test 4) is **a.** 140 mph

ANSWER TO QUESTION 4 (PRACTICE TEST 4)

$$Time = \frac{distance}{speed} = \frac{40}{30} = 1.33333 \text{ hours per day}$$

For 5 days, multiply this by 5:

$$1.333333 \times 5 = 6.666666667 \text{ hours}$$

The '0.666666667' part of the hours needs to be converted into minutes. To convert hours into minutes, multiply the hours by 60 as shown below:

$$0.6666666667 \text{ hours in minutes} = 0.666666667 \times 60$$

$$= 40 \text{ minutes}$$

This means that every day Emma spends 6 hours and 40 minutes going to work and back for 5 days a week.

The answer to question 4 (Practice Test 4) is **a.** 6 hours 40 minutes

ANSWER TO QUESTION 5 (PRACTICE TEST 4)

$$Time = \frac{distance}{speed} = \frac{24}{96} = 0.25 \ hours$$

To convert hours into minutes, multiply the hours by 60.

$$0.25 \ hours \ in \ minutes = 0.25 \times 60 = 15 \ minutes$$

The answer to question 5 (Practice Test 4) is **b.** 15 minutes

ANSWER TO QUESTION 6 (PRACTICE TEST 4)

The speed is given in miles per hour. This means that time needs to be in hours. Alternatively, miles per hour can be converted into miles per minute, simply divide the miles per hour by 60 and only then can time in minutes be used in the formula below.

To convert minutes into hours:

$$20 \ minutes = 20 \div 60 = 0.3333333333\ldots\ldots \ hours$$

$$Distance = speed \times time$$

$$= 42 \times 0.33333333\ldots.$$

$$= 14 \ miles$$

To convert miles per hour into miles per minute:

$$42 \ mph = 42 \div 60$$

$$= 0.7 \ miles \ per \ minute$$

$$Distance = speed \times time$$

$$= 0.7 \times 20$$

$$= 14 \ miles$$

Both methods give the same answer – the key is to use the correct units!

The answer to question 6 (Practice Test 4) is **a.** 14 miles

ANSWER TO QUESTION 7 (PRACTICE TEST 4)

One quarter as a decimal is 0.25 and as a fraction is 1/4. To calculate how many people over 50 years of age are arrested, multiply either the decimal or fraction (whichever you find easiest to use) by the amount of people arrested which is 20,600.

$$\textit{Number of people over } 50 \textit{ arrested} = 20,600 \times 0.25$$

$$= 5,150 \textit{ people}$$

The answer to question 7 (Practice Test 4) is **e.** 5,150

ANSWER TO QUESTION 8 (PRACTICE TEST 4)

$$2 \textit{ out of } 10 = \frac{2}{10} = 0.2$$

As there were 2 out of 10 entrants that won at a dog show multiply this by the total number of entrant to find how many won.

$$0.2 \times 100 = 20 \textit{ winners}$$

The answer to question 8 (Practice Test 4) is **c.** 20 winners

ANSWER TO QUESTION 9 (PRACTICE TEST 4)

The perimeter can be calculated by adding together all the outside lengths of the shape.

Perimeter = 3.1 cm + 3.4 cm + 3.8 cm + 3.7 cm + 3.8 cm + 3.1 cm
      + 3.7 cm + 3.4 cm

    = 28 cm

The answer to question 9 (Practice Test 4) is **b.** 28 cm

ANSWER TO QUESTION 10 (PRACTICE TEST 4)

$21,000m^2 \div 700$ employees $= 30m^2$ per employee

The answer to question 10 (Practice Test 4) is **b.** $30m^2$

ANSWER TO QUESTION 11 (PRACTICE TEST 4)

£42 is already paid for towards the army boots. Therefore you will need to pay:

$$£112 - £42 = £70$$

The answer to question 11 (Practice Test 4) is **e.** £70

ANSWER TO QUESTION 12 (PRACTICE TEST 4)

$$Amount\ left = £13 - £4.37$$

$$= £8.63$$

The answer to question 12 (Practice Test 4) is **c.** £8.63

ANSWER TO QUESTION 13 (PRACTICE TEST 4)

$$Cost\ of\ 24\ boxes = 24 \times £4.10$$

$$= £98.40$$

The answer to question 13 (Practice Test 4) is **e.** £98.40

ANSWER TO QUESTION 14 (PRACTICE TEST 4)

36 out of 200 are over the legal limit. As a fraction this is 36/200. To convert a fraction into a percentage, multiply the fraction by 100.

This can easily be achieved using a calculator by doing the following:

$$36 \div 200 = 0.18$$

Now multiply 0.18 by 100 to give 18%

$$0.18 \times 100 = 18\%$$

The answer to question 14 (Practice Test 4) is **b.** 18%

ANSWER TO QUESTION 15 (PRACTICE TEST 4)

30% are female which means that 70% are male (because percentages add up to 100%). To convert 70% into a decimal, divide it by 100.

$$70\% = 70 \div 100 = 0.7$$

Now multiply this by 15,000 to find how many male paramedics are recruited in Scotland each year.

$$15{,}000 \times 0.7 = 10{,}500 \text{ } \textit{male paramedics}$$

The answer to question 15 (Practice Test 4) is **c.** 10,500

ANSWER TO QUESTION 16 (PRACTICE TEST 4)

$$\textit{Average} = \frac{\textit{Sum of the individual ages}}{\textit{Number of children}}$$

$$= \frac{10 + 11 + 12 + 13 + 14}{5}$$

$$= \frac{60}{5}$$

$$= 12$$

The answer to question 16 (Practice Test 4) is **c.** 12

ANSWER TO QUESTION 17 (PRACTICE TEST 4)

$$\textit{Cost to buy 26 jars of jam} = 26 \times £1.15$$

$$= £29.90$$

The answer to question 17 (Practice Test 4) is **e.** £29.90

ANSWER TO QUESTION 18 (PRACTICE TEST 4)

One lorry contains 635 boxes. 3 lorries would contain three times the amount one lorry contains.

$$Number\ of\ boxes\ in\ 3\ lorries = 635 \times 3$$

$$= 1{,}905\ boxes$$

The answer to question 18 (Practice Test 4) is **d.** 1,905

ANSWER TO QUESTION 19 (PRACTICE TEST 4)

25 sweets cost £4.00. To find the cost of one sweet, divide the price by the number of sweets.

$$Cost\ per\ sweet = £4 \div 25 = £0.16$$

The answer to question 19 (Practice Test 4) is **b.** £0.16

ANSWER TO QUESTION 20 (PRACTICE TEST 4)

$$Average\ miles\ walked\ per\ day = \frac{725\ miles}{5}$$

$$= 145\ miles$$

The answer to question 20 (Practice Test 4) is **a.** 145 miles

ANSWER TO QUESTION 21 (PRACTICE TEST 4)

$$Average = \frac{£19 + £22 + £21.75 + £25.25}{4}$$

$$= £88/4$$

$$= £22$$

The answer to question 21 (Practice Test 4) is **d.** £22

ANSWER TO QUESTION 22 (PRACTICE TEST 4)

To split £520,000 equally into 13 parts, divide the two as shown below:

Profit each individual makes = £520,000 ÷ 13

= £40,000

The answer to question 22 (Practice Test 4) is **d.** £40,000.

PRACTICE TEST 5

Q1. At a football tournament there are 15 teams. Each team has a squad of twenty players. How many players are there in total?

    a. 200   **b.** 300   **c.** 400   **d.** 450   **e.** 500

Q2. The total number of hours worked by employees in a week is 390. If there are 13 employees, how many hours per work does each person work assuming they all work the same number of hours?

    a. 3 hours   **b.** 20 hours   **c.** 30 hours   **d.** 45 hours   **e.** 60 hours

Q3. The diagram below shows a playing field and a sand pit. Calculate the area of the playing field using the information displayed.

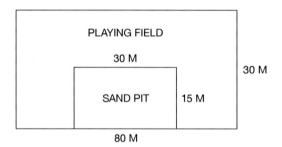

    a. 950 m²   **b.** 1,400 m²   **c.** 1,950 m²   **d.** 2,400 m²   **e.** 2,850 m²

Q4. Hampshire Police operate a three-shift working pattern each day. Each shift has to have 24 police officers on duty. How many officers are required for a week's work, Monday to Friday?

    a. 36   **b.** 480   **c.** 420   **d.** 504   **e.** 360

Q5. You need to measure the perimeter of a square house. You know that one side of the house measures 15.5 metres. What is the perimeter of the house?

    a. 52 metres   **b.** 62 metres   **c.** 63 metres
    d. 64 metres   **e.** 66 metres

Q6. A road worker has to put some marker cones out along a stretch of road. The road is 240 metres long and cones have to be placed 1.5 metres apart. How many cones will the road worker need?

    a. 150   **b.** 160   **c.** 165   **d.** 170   **e.** 180

Q7. The school run in Milton Keynes takes 3 minutes if you drive at a speed of 30 mph. How far away is the school?

    a. 1.5 miles   **b.** 2 miles   **c.** 3 miles   **d.** 5.5 miles   **e.** 10 miles

Q8. You are flying at 240 mph. How far have you travelled in 12 minutes?

    a. 24 miles   **b.** 48 miles   **c.** 36 miles   **d.** 20 miles   **e.** 40 miles

Q9. You have arrived at an RTA (Road Traffic Accident) and immediately call for an ambulance. The ambulance is 12 miles from your current location. You have told the ambulance that you need it here in 5 minutes. What speed must the ambulance drive at to get to the RTA on time?

    a. 60 mph   **b.** 140 mph   **c.** 50 mph   **d.** 144 mph   **e.** 132 mph

Q10. There are 18 strawberries in a punnet. In a shop there are 12 punnets. How many strawberries are there in total?

    a. 132   **b.** 162   **c.** 316   **d.** 432   **e.** 216

Q11. You find a purse in the street. It contains a £10 note, a £5 note, four £2 coins, three £1 coins, a 50p coin, four 2p coins and a penny. How much is there in the purse?

    a. £22.59   **b.** £22.49   **c.** £24.69   **d.** £25.69   **e.** £26.59

Q12. A car park in Warrington issues 15 parking fines a week, each costing £60. How much does the car park make from fines every 4 weeks?

    a. £1,800   **b.** £2,600   **c.** £3,600   **d.** £3,800   **e.** £4,800

Q13. Mary goes food shopping 3 times a week. How many times does she go food shopping in a year?

    a. 156   **b.** 158   **c.** 166   **d.** 226   **e.** 256

Q14. The plan below shows a layout of your garden and vegetable plot. You want to lay decking over half of the garden. What area will the decking cover?

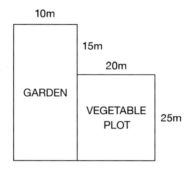

    a. 20 m²   **b.** 100 m²   **c.** 125 m²   **d.** 175 m²   **e.** 200 m²

Q15. 15% of the vegetable plot is used to grow carrots. Using the above diagram calculate what area of the vegetable plot is used to grow carrots?

    a. 25 m²   **b.** 37.5 m²   **c.** 48 m²   **d.** 50 m²   **e.** 75 m²

Q16. At Lowbridge High School there are 180 students taking exams. 60 of these students gain A to C grades. What is this as a fraction?

    a. 1/4   **b.** 1/3   **c.** 2/3   **d.** 1/6   **e.** 1/5

Q17. Your family own 5 cars. 3 of the cars are red. What is this as a percentage?

    a. 30%   **b.** 40%   **c.** 60%   **d.** 65%   **e.** 70%

Q18. Whilst shopping I spend £1.60, £2.35, £5.60 and 74p. How much have I spent in total?

    a. £10.39   **b.** £10.29   **c.** £10.49   **d.** £10.59   **e.** £11.29

Q19. A car ownership survey discovered that out of 10,000 cars, 2,500 were Fords. What is this as a percentage?

 a. 20% **b.** 25% **c.** 30% **d.** 35% **e.** 40%

Q20. A motorbike is speeding at 180 mph. How far does it travel in 10 minutes?

 a. 60 miles **b.** 40 miles **c.** 30 miles **d.** 25 miles **e.** 20 miles

Q21. A train is travelling at a speed of 80 mph. The distance between station A and station B is 200 miles. How long will it take to get from station A to station B?

 a. 2 hours 15 minutes **b.** 2 hours 20 minutes **c.** 2 hours 35 minutes
 d. 2 hours 40 minutes **e.** 2 hours 30 minutes

Q22. You are running late for work and you have 30 minutes to get there on time. Your work is 25 miles away. What speed do you have to drive at so as not to be late?

 a. 75 mph **b.** 45 mph **c.** 50 mph **d.** 30 mph **e.** 15 mph

Q23. What speed would you need to travel at in order to cover 180 miles in 20 minutes?

 a. 360 mph **b.** 540 mph **c.** 270 mph **d.** 90 mph **e.** 100 mph

ANSWERS TO PRACTICE TEST 5

ANSWER TO QUESTION 1 (PRACTICE TEST 5)

15 teams with 20 players in each team.

$$Total\ players = 15 \times 20 = 300\ players$$

The answer to question 1 (Practice Test 5) is **b.** 300 players

ANSWER TO QUESTION 2 (PRACTICE TEST 5)

The total hours worked by all the employees in a week is 390. As there are 13 employees, divide this by 13 to find the number of hours each person works.

$$Hours\ each\ person\ works = 390 \div 13 = 30\ hours$$

The answer to question 2 (Practice Test 5) is **c.** 30 hours

ANSWER TO QUESTION 3 (PRACTICE TEST 5)

The total area (Playing Field and Sand Pit combined) can be calculated by multiplying the length and width of the outer rectangle.

$$Area\ of\ playing\ field\ and\ Sand\ Pit = 30m \times 80m$$

$$= 2400m^2$$

If the area of the sand pit is subtracted from the total area, then only the area of the playing field will remain.

$$Area\ of\ Sand\ Pit = 30m \times 15m$$

$$= 450m^2$$

$$Area\ of\ playing\ field = Area\ of\ playing\ field\ and\ Sand\ Pit - Area\ of\ Sand\ Pit$$

$$= 2400m^2 - 450m^2$$

$$= 1,950m^2$$

The answer to question 3 (Practice Test 5) is **c.** 1,950m²

ANSWER TO QUESTION 4 (PRACTICE TEST 5)

There are 3 shifts in a day. 1 shift has 24 police officers on duty. 3 shifts will have 3 times the amount of officers.

Total officers in 3 shifts = 72 officers

Therefore, 72 officers are required per day. For 5 days (Monday to Friday), multiply this by 5:

$$72 \times 5 = 360 \text{ officers}$$

The answer to question 4 (Practice Test 5) is **e.** 360

ANSWER TO QUESTION 5 (PRACTICE TEST 5)

A square means that both height and width are the same measurement. If one side of the square is 15.5 metres, all 4 sides of the square will be 15.5 metres.

Perimeter of the house = 15.5m + 15.5m + 15.5m + 15.5m

$$= 62 \text{ m}$$

ANSWER TO QUESTION 6 (PRACTICE TEST 5)

The cones are placed 1.5 metres apart equally for a distance of 240 metres.

Amount of cones the road worker needs = 240 metres ÷ 1.5 metres

$$= 160 \text{ cones}$$

The answer to question 6 (Practice Test 5) is **b.** 160 cones

ANSWER TO QUESTION 7 (PRACTICE TEST 5)

A time of 3 minutes in hours = 3 ÷ 60

$$= 0.05 \text{ hours}$$

A speed of 30 miles per hour in miles per minutes = 30 ÷ 60

$$= 0.5 \text{ miles per minute}$$

For this question, either 3 minutes can be used as the time along with a speed of 0.5 miles per minute, or a time of 0.05 hours along with a speed of 30 mph can be used.

Do not confuse the two or the answer will be incorrect!

Using 0.5 miles per minute and 3 minutes

$$Distance = Speed \times Time$$

$$= 0.5 \ miles \ per \ minute \times 3 \ minutes$$

$$= 1.5 \ miles$$

Using 0.05 hours and a speed of 30 miles per hour

$$Distance = Speed \times Time$$

$$= 30 \ miles \ per \ hour \times 0.05 \ hours$$

$$= 1.5 \ miles$$

Both give the same answer.

The answer to question 7 (Practice Test 5) is **a.** 1.5 miles

ANSWER TO QUESTION 8 (PRACTICE TEST 5)

$$A \ time \ of \ 12 \ minutes \ in \ hours = 12 \div 60$$

$$= 0.2 \ hours$$

$$A \ speed \ of \ 240 \ miles \ per \ hour \ in \ miles \ per \ minutes = 240 \div 60$$

$$= 4 \ miles \ per \ minute$$

For this question, either 12 minutes can be used as the time along with a speed of 4 miles per minute, or a time of 0.2 hours along with a speed of 240 mph can be used.

Do not confuse the two or the answer will be incorrect!

Using 4 miles per minute and 12 minutes

$$Distance = Speed \times Time$$

$$= 4 \ miles \ per \ minute \times 12 \ minutes$$

$$= 48 \ miles$$

Using 0.2 hours and a speed of 240 miles per hour

$$Distance = Speed \times Time$$

$$= 240 \ miles \ per \ hour \times 0.2 \ hours$$

$$= 48 \ miles$$

Both give the same answer.

The answer to question 8 (Practice Test 5) is **b.** 48 miles

ANSWER TO QUESTION 9 (PRACTICE TEST 5).

$$Speed = \frac{distance}{time}$$

$$= \frac{12 \ miles}{5 \ minutes}$$

$$= 2.4 \ miles \ per \ minutes$$

To convert miles per minute into miles per hour, multiply the miles per minute by 60.

$$2.4 \ miles \ per \ minute \ in \ miles \ per \ hour = 144 \ mph$$

The answer to question 9 (Practice Test 5) is **d.** 144 mph

ANSWER TO QUESTION 10 (PRACTICE TEST 5)

$$Number \ of \ strawberries \ in \ total = 12 \times 18$$

$$= 216 \ strawberries$$

The answer to question 10 (Practice Test 5) is **e.** 216

ANSWER TO QUESTION 11 (PRACTICE TEST 5)

Remember to convert pence into pounds by dividing the pence by 100.

$$50p = £0.50 \quad 2p = £0.02 \quad 1p = £0.01$$

$$Total \ in \ the \ pure = £10 + £5 + £2 + £2 + £2 + £2 + £1 + £1 + £1 + £0.5$$
$$+ £0.02 + £0.02 + £0.02 + £0.02 + £0.01$$

$$= £ \ 26.59$$

The answer to question 11 (Practice Test 5) is **e.** £26.59

ANSWER TO QUESTION 12 (PRACTICE TEST 5)

15 parking fines a week costing £60 a fine amounts to:

$$15 \times £60 = £900 \ a \ week$$

In 4 weeks, this would be four times the amount of fines paid in a week:

$$£900 \times 4 = £3,600$$

The answer to question 12 (Practice test 5) is **c.** £3,600

ANSWER TO QUESTION 13 (PRACTICE TEST 5)

There are 52 weeks in a year. If Mary goes food shopping 3 times a week, in a year this would be:

$$52 \times 3 = 156$$

The answer to question 13 (Practice Test 5) is **a.** 156

ANSWER TO QUESTION 14 (PRACTICE TEST 5)

The garden has a length of 35m and a width of 10m (see image below). The area of the garden is given by:

$$Area \ of \ garden = 35m \times 10m$$

$$= 350m^2$$

Half of this area is $350 \div 2 = 175m^2$ and this is the area the decking will cover.

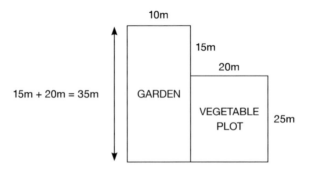

The answer to question 14 (Practice Test 5) is **d.** 175m²

ANSWER TO QUESTION 15 (PRACTICE TEST 5)

The area of the vegetable plot in the previous question is:

$$Area\ of\ vegetable\ plot = 20m \times 25m$$

$$= 500m^2$$

$$15\%\ as\ a\ decimal = 15 \div 100$$

$$= 0.15$$

$$15\%\ of\ 500m^2 = 0.15 \times 500m^2$$

$$= 75m^2$$

The answer to question 15 (Practice Test 5) is **e.** 75m²

ANSWER TO QUESTION 16 (PRACTICE TEST 5)

As a fraction this is 60/180. Now ask yourself how many times 60 goes into 180. Or if this is too hard for you, imagine that both the zeros have cancelled each other out so that the fraction is now:

$$\frac{60}{180} = \frac{6}{18}$$

Now ask yourself how many 6's go into 18. The correct answer is 3. The fraction can now be written as:

$$\frac{6}{18} = \frac{1}{3}$$

The answer to question 16 (Practice Test 5) is **b.** 1/3

ANSWER TO QUESTION 17 (PRACTICE TEST 5)

3 out of 5 cars are red. As a fraction this is 3/5 which is 0.6 as a decimal

To convert a fraction or decimal into a percentage, multiply it by 100.

$$0.6 \times 100 = 60\%$$

The answer to question 17 (Practice Test 5) is **c.** 60%

ANSWER TO QUESTION 18 (PRACTICE TEST 5)

$$Total\ spent = £1.60 + £2.35 + £5.60 + £0.74$$

$$= £10.29$$

The answer to question 18 (Practice Test 5) is **b.** £10.29

ANSWER TO QUESTION 19 (PRACTICE TEST 5)

As a fraction this can be written as 2500/10000. To convert this into a decimal do the following calculation:

$$2500 ÷ 10000 = 0.25$$

As a decimal this is 0.25. To convert a decimal into a percentage, multiply it by 100.

$$0.25 × 100 = 25\%$$

The answer to question 19 (Practice Test 5) is **b.** 25%

ANSWER TO QUESTION 20 (PRACTICE TEST 5)

$$A\ speed\ of\ 180\ miles\ per\ hour\ in\ miles\ per\ minutes = 180 ÷ 60$$

$$= 3\ miles\ per\ minute$$

$$Distance = Speed × Time$$

$$= 3\ miles\ per\ minute × 10\ minutes$$

$$= 30\ miles$$

The answer to question 20 (Practice Test 5) is **c.** 30 miles

ANSWER TO QUESTION 21 (PRACTICE TEST 5)

$$Time = \frac{distance}{speed}$$

$$= \frac{200\ miles}{80\ mph}$$

$$= 2.5 \text{ hours}$$

0.5 of an hour is half an hour which is 30 minutes. This means it took 2 hours 30 minutes to get from station A to station B.

The answer to question 21 (Practice Test 5) is **e.** 2 hours 30 minutes

ANSWER TO QUESTION 22 (PRACTICE TEST 5)

$$30 \text{ minutes in hours} = 30 \div 60$$

$$= 0.5 \text{ hours}$$

$$Speed = \frac{distance}{time}$$

$$= \frac{25 \text{ miles}}{0.5 \text{ hours}}$$

$$= 50 \text{ mph}$$

The answer to question 22 (Practice Test 5) is **c.** 50 mph

ANSWER TO QUESTION 23 (PRACTICE TEST 5)

The easiest method of solving this question is by keeping the time in minutes rather than hours and then finally converting miles per minutes into miles per hour.

$$Speed = \frac{distance}{time}$$

$$= \frac{180 \text{ miles}}{20 \text{ minutes}}$$

$$= 9 \text{ miles per minute}$$

To convert miles per minute into miles per hour multiply by 60.

$$9 \text{ miles per minute in miles per hour} = 9 \times 60$$

$$= 540 \text{ mph}$$

The answer to question 23 (Practice Test 5) is **b.** 540 mph

PRACTICE TEST 6

Q1. As a sales representative you cover 360 miles a day. Over an 8-hour shift, what is your average speed for the day?

    a. 50 mph   **b.** 60 mph   **c.** 48 mph   **d.** 45 mph   **e.** 46 mph

Q2. A journey takes 2 hours and 30 minutes. You have been travelling at a speed of 70 mph. How far have you travelled?

    a. 160 miles   **b.** 170 miles   **c.** 175 miles   **d.** 185 miles   **e.** 190 miles

Q3. A garage is selling three used cars. The mileage on the first is 119,500; the mileage on the second is 140,500; the mileage on the third in 160,000. What is the average mileage of the three used cars?

    a. 140,000   **b.** 142,000   **c.** 145,000   **d.** 150,000   **e.** 135,000

Q4. At a restaurant you and your friend buy a king prawn salad (£6.95), some salmon fish cakes (£5.95), steak and chips (£11.50), chicken and chips (£10.25) and a chocolate cake (£3.95). You agree to split the bill equally. How much do you both pay?

    a. £19.50   **b.** £19.40   **c.** £19.30   **d.** £19.20   **e.** £19.10

Q5. In a restaurant you and your friend buy a salad (£3.95), scallops (£6.95), steak and chips (£12.60), chicken and chips (£9.15) and ice cream (£1.95). You agree to split the bill equally, how much do you both pay?

    a. £17.35   **b.** £18.40   **c.** £17.60   **d.** £15.30   **e.** £17.30

Q6. A company adds up the total number of sick days had by its employees. Out of the 52 weeks in a year it is calculated that, in total, employees have 13 weeks off sick. What is this as a percentage?

    a. 25%   **b.** 20%   **c.** 15%   **d.** 10%   **e.** 5%

Q7. Using the diagram below, calculate the perimeter of the lily bed.

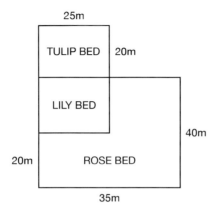

a. 70 m   **b.** 75 m   **c.** 90 m   **d.** 95 m   **e.** 100 m

Q8. A bag contains 5 litres of compost soil. You calculate that 5 litres of compost will cover an area of 2.5 m. Using the above diagram calculate how many bags of soil you will need to fill the tulip bed.

a. 20 bags   **b.** 100 bags   **c.** 200 bags   **d.** 250 bags   **e.** 400 bags

Q9. If the air ambulance flies at a speed of 120 mph for 12 minutes, how far has it travelled?

a. 48 miles   **b.** 26 miles   **c.** 12 miles   **d.** 24 miles   **e.** 6 miles

Q10. A bus drives for 4 hours covering a total distance of 240 miles. What was his average speed in miles per hour?

a. 120 mph   **b.** 30 mph   **c.** 40 mph   **d.** 60 mph   **e.** 50 mph

Q11. Five out of one hundred rugby players are injured every year.

What is this as a fraction?

a. 1/5   **b.** 1/20   **c.** 1/30   **d.** 2/50   **e.** 1/4

Q12. School dinners cost £4.75 each, and 200 children have dinners each day. How much is made from school dinners per day?

    a. £550   **b.** £750   **c.** £850   **d.** £950   **e.** £1,050

Q13. You have a meeting at 0900hrs. You leave your house at 0840hrs. The meeting location from your house is 20 miles away. It will take you 5 minutes to walk from your car to the meeting room. What speed must you drive at to ensure you are on time?

    a. 70 mph   **b.** 65 mph   **c.** 80 mph   **d.** 75 mph   **e.** 60 mph

Q14. Farmer Sid collects bales of hay during his autumn harvest. In his first field he collects 43, in his second field he collects 62, in his third field he collects 13 and in his fourth field he collects 42. What is the average number of hay bales he collects from his fields?

    a. 39   **b.** 40   **c.** 41   **d.** 42   **e.** 37

Q15. There are four new firefighter recruits named Mark, Laura, Ryan and Amy. Mark is 2 metres tall, Laura is 1.7 metres tall, Ryan is 1.8 metres tall, and Amy is 1.5 metres tall. What is the average height of the recruits in metres?

    a. 1.77 metres   **b.** 1.68 metres   **c.** 1.62 metres
    d. 1.70 metres   **e.** 1.75 metres

Q16. Below is a bar chart showing daily book sales for four stores. How many books in total does Jay's Books sell.

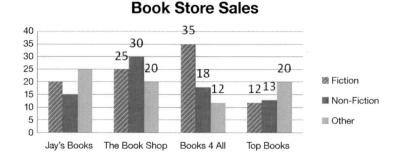

    a. 40   **b.** 45   **c.** 50   **d.** 55   **e.** 60

Q17. What, on average, is the total amount of books sold at The Book Shop and Top Books?

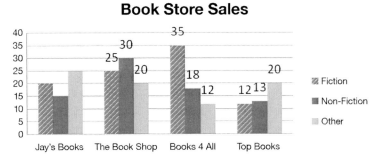

Book Store Sales

a. 50   b. 55   c. 60   d. 75   e. 90

Q18. Whilst shopping you buy 6 items. You buy a steak costing £12.50, some vegetables costing £5.75, some cereal costing £1.21, some wine costing £10, some shampoo costing 42p and finally some sweets costing 12p. What is the average cost of the items you buy?

a. £4   b. £5   c. £6   d. £7   e. £8

Q19. The distance between A and B is 140 miles. It takes you 4 hours to drive the distance. What speed have you been travelling at?

a. 70 mph   b. 40 mph   c. 35 mph   d. 30 mph   e. 25 mph

Q20. You must arrive at work at 0900hrs. Your house is 6 miles from work. If you were to drive at 30 mph, what time would you need to leave the house to arrive at work on time?

a. 0847hrs   b. 0857hrs   c. 0848hrs   d. 0842hrs   e. 0838hrs

Q21. On a Saturday night the police arrest 40 people. 22 are arrested for being drunk and disorderly, 10 are arrested for assault and 8 are arrested for drink driving. What percentage have been arrested for drink driving?

a. 2%   b. 5%   c. 10%   d. 20%   e. 25%

Q22. During a daily patrol you average 12 miles at 3 mph. How long would it take to do a 14-mile patrol?

    a. 4 hours 50 minutes   **b.** 4 hours 45 minutes   **c.** 4 hours 20 minutes
    d. 4 hours 35 minutes   **e.** 4 hours 40 minutes

Q23. A train is travelling from Birmingham to Glasgow covering a distance of 390 miles. If the train's speed is 90 mph, how long does the train journey last?

    a. 4 hours 20 minutes   **b.** 4 hours 40 minutes   **c.** 4 hours 10 minutes
    d. 4 hours 15 minutes   **e.** 4 hours 30 minutes

Q24. You have 225 bags of sugar. If 15 bags of sugar fit in a box, how many boxes would you have in total?

    a. 10   **b.** 12   **c.** 13   **d.** 15   **e.** 20

ANSWERS TO PRACTICE TEST 6

ANSWER TO QUESTION 1 (PRACTICE TEST 6)

$$Average\ Speed = \frac{distance}{time}$$

$$= \frac{360\ miles}{8\ hours}$$

$$= 45\ mph$$

The answer to question 1 (practice test 6) is **d.** 45 mph

ANSWER TO QUESTION 2 (PRACTICE TEST 6)

2 hours 30 minutes is equivalent to 2.5 hours

$$Distance = Speed \times Time$$

$$= 70\ mph \times 2.5\ minutes$$

$$= 175\ miles$$

The answer to question 2 (Practice Test 6) is **c.** 175 miles

ANSWER TO QUESTION 3 (PRACTICE TEST 6)

$$Average\ mileage = \frac{Total\ mileage\ of\ all\ 3\ cars\ combined}{Number\ of\ cars}$$

$$= \frac{119{,}500 + 140{,}500 + 160{,}000}{3}$$

$$= \frac{420{,}000}{3}$$

$$= 140{,}000$$

The answer to question 3 (Practice Test 6) is **a.** 140,000

ANSWER TO QUESTION 4 (PRACTICE TEST 6)

Total bill = £6.95 + £5.95 + £11.50 + £10.25 + £3.95

= £38.60

If you and your friend equally split the bill then each person pays half this amount:

Amount each person pays = £38.60 ÷ 2

= £19.30

The answer to question 4 (Practice Test 6) is **c.** £19.30

ANSWER TO QUESTION 5 (PRACTICE TEST 6)

Total bill = £3.95 + £6.95 + £12.60 + £9.15 + £1.95

= £34.60

If you and your friend equally split the bill then each person pays half this amount:

Amount each person pays = £34.60 ÷ 2

= £17.30

The answer to question 5 (Practice Test 6) is **e.** £17.30

ANSWER TO QUESTION 6 (PRACTICE TEST 6)

As a decimal, 13 out of 52 weeks = 13 ÷ 52 = 0.25

To convert a decimal into a percentage, multiply it by 100%:

0.25 × 100 = 25%

The answer to question 6 (Practice Test 6) is **a.** 25%

ANSWER TO QUESTION 7 (PRACTICE TEST 6)

From the diagram, the width of the Lily bed is the same as that of the tulip bed. The height of the lily bed is 20m because from the bottom of the rose bed to the start of the lily bed is 20m.

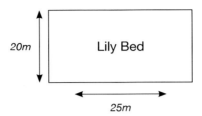

The perimeter of the lily bed can be found by adding together the measurement of all the four sides of the lily bed.

Perimeter of Lily bed = 25m + 25m + 20m + 20m

= 90m

The answer to question 7 (Practice Test 6) is **c.** 90m

ANSWER TO QUESTION 8 (PRACTICE TEST 6)

To calculate area, multiply length by width. Remember that the units of area are always squared e.g. metres squared, centimetres squared etc.

Area of Lily Bed = 25m × 20m = 500m^2

If 5 litre bag of compost covers an area of 2.5m^2 only, how many bags will it take to cover 500m^2? This can be found by division:

Amount of compost bags required to cover 500m^2 = 500m^2 ÷ 2.5m^2

= 200 bags

The answer to question 8 (Practice Test 6) is **c.** 200 bags

ANSWER TO QUESTION 9 (PRACTICE TEST 6)

12 *minutes = 0.2 hours*

Distance = Speed × Time

= 120 mph × 0.2 hours

= 24 miles

The answer to question 9 (Practice Test 6) is **d.** 24 miles

ANSWER TO QUESTION 10 (PRACTICE TEST 6)

$$Average\ Speed = \frac{distance}{time}$$

$$= \frac{240\ miles}{4\ hours}$$

$$= 60\ mph$$

The answer to question 10 (practice test 6) is **d.** 60 mph

ANSWER TO QUESTION 11 (PRACTICE TEST 6)

5 out of 100 as a fraction is:

$$\frac{5}{100}$$

This can be simplified further. Ask yourself how many times 5 goes into 100. The answer is 20.

$$\frac{5}{100} = \frac{1}{20}$$

Alternatively, both the top (numerator) and bottom (denominator) of the fraction could have been divided by 5 to give the same answer.

The answer to question 11 (Practice Test 6) is **b.** 1/20

ANSWER TO QUESTION 12 (PRACTICE TEST 6)

$$200 \times £4.75 = £950\ per\ day$$

The answer to question 12 (Practice Test 6) is **d.** £950

ANSWER TO QUESTION 13 (PRACTICE TEST 6)

If it takes you 5 minutes to walk from your car to the meeting room then you must arrive at 08.55. If you leave at 08.40, this leaves 15 minutes to get there by car.

$$15\ minutes\ in\ hours = 15 \div 60$$

$$= 0.25\ hours$$

$$Speed = \frac{distance}{time}$$

$$= \frac{20\ miles}{0.25\ hours}$$

$$= 80\ mph$$

You must drive at 80 mph to ensure you are on time.

The answer to question 13 (Practice Test 6) is **c.** 80 mph

ANSWER TO QUESTION 14 (PRACTICE TEST 6)

$$Average = \frac{Total\ amount\ collected}{Number\ of\ fields\ collected\ from}$$

$$= \frac{43 + 62 + 13 + 42}{4}$$

$$= \frac{160}{4}$$

$$= 40$$

The answer to question 14 (Practice Test 6) is **b.** 40

ANSWER TO QUESTION 15 (PRACTICE TEST 6)

To find an average height, add all the heights together and divide by the number of people:

$$Average\ height = \frac{Total\ of\ all\ heights\ added\ together}{Number\ of\ heights\ being\ measured}$$

$$= \frac{2 + 1.7 + 1.8 + 1.5}{4}$$

$$= \frac{7}{4}$$

$$= 1.75\ metres$$

The answer to question 15 (Practice Test 6) is **e.** 1.75 metres

ANSWER TO QUESTION 16 (PRACTICE TEST 6)

Looking at the graph, Jay's books sells 20 Fiction books, 15 nonfiction books and 25 books in the 'other' category.

In total Jay's books sells: 20 + 15 + 25 = 60 *books*

The answer to question 16 (Practice Test 6) is **e.** 60

ANSWER TO QUESTION 17 (PRACTICE TEST 6)

The book shop *sells* 25 + 30 + 20 = 75 *books*

Top Books *sell* 12 + 13 + 20 = 45 *books*

$$Average = \frac{75 + 45}{2}$$

$$= \frac{120}{2}$$

$$= 60 \ books$$

The answer to question 17 (Practice Test 6) is **c.** 60

ANSWER TO QUESTION 18 (PRACTICE TEST 6)

$$Average \ cost = \frac{Total \ Cost}{Number \ of \ items \ purchased}$$

$$= \frac{£12.50 + £5.75 + £1.21 + £10 + £0.42 + £0.12}{6}$$

$$= \frac{£30}{6}$$

$$= £5$$

The answer to question 18 (Practice test 6) is **b.** £5

ANSWER TO QUESTION 19 (PRACTICE TEST 6)

$$Average\ Speed = \frac{distance}{time}$$

$$= \frac{140\ miles}{4\ hours}$$

$$= 35\ mph$$

The answer to question 19 (Practice Test 6) is **c.** 35 mph

ANSWER TO QUESTION 20 (PRACTICE TEST 6)

$$Time = \frac{distance}{speed}$$

$$= \frac{6\ miles}{30\ mph}$$

$$= 0.2\ hours$$

$$0.2\ hours\ in\ minutes = 0.2 \times 60$$

$$= 12\ minutes$$

Therefore to arrive at work on time, you would need to leave at least 12 minutes before the start time of 0900 hrs. This would mean the latest time you could leave is 0848 hrs.

The answer to question 20 (Practice Test 6) is **c.** 0848hrs

ANSWER TO QUESTION 21 (PRACTICE TEST 6)

8 out of 40 people are arrested for drink driving. As a fraction this is 8/40. To convert a fraction into a percentage, multiply the fraction by 100. This can easily be achieved using a calculator by doing the following:

$$8 \div 40 = 0.2$$

Now multiply 0.2 by 100 to give 20%

$$0.2 \times 100 = 20\%$$

The answer to question 21 (Practice Test 6) is **d.** 20%

ANSWER TO QUESTION 22 (PRACTICE TEST 6)

$$\textit{Time to do a 12 mile patrol} = \frac{distance}{speed}$$

$$= \frac{12\ miles}{3\ mph}$$

$$= 4\ hours$$

It takes 4 hours to cover 12 miles. To calculate how long it takes to cover 14 miles use the following cross multiplication method.

Label the time taken to cover 14 miles as '*x*':

Time takenMiles Covered

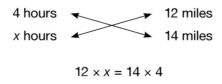

4 hours   12 miles

x hours   14 miles

$$12 \times x = 14 \times 4$$

Now find *x*:

$$12x = 56$$

$$x = 56/12$$

$$= 4.66666667$$

The '0.66666667' part of 4.66666667needs to converted into minutes because 4.66666667 does not mean 4 hours 66666667 minutes!

To convert 0.66666667hours into minutes, multiply by 60:

$$0.66666667 \times 60 = 40\ \textit{minutes}$$

In total, the time taken to cover 14 miles is 4 hours and 40 minutes.

The answer to question 22 (Practice Test 6) is **e.** 4 hours 40 minutes

ANSWER TO QUESTION 23 (PRACTICE TEST 6)

$$Time = \frac{distance}{speed}$$

$$= \frac{390\ miles}{90\ mph}$$

$$= 4.333333\ hours$$

To convert hours into minutes multiply by 60. This is necessary to calculate what 0.3333333... hours is in minutes because 4.333333... hours does not mean 4 hours and 333333333333...... minutes

$$0.333333333...hours \times 60 = 20\ minutes$$

The train journey lasted 4 hours and 20 minutes.

The answer to question 23 (Practice Test 6) is **a.** 4 hours 20 minutes

ANSWER TO QUESTION 24 (PRACTICE TEST 6)

$$Boxes\ in\ total = 225 \div 15$$

$$= 15\ boxes$$

The answer to question 24 (Practice Test 6) is **d.** 15

PRACTICE TEST 7

Q1. An aircraft travels at a speed of 120 miles per hour over a total distance of 240 miles. How long does the journey take?

    a. 2 hours   **b.** 4 hours   **c.** 3 hours
    d. 2 hours 30 minutes   **e.** 1 hour

Q2. How long does it take to drive 20 miles if you drive at a speed of 30 mph?

    a. 1 hour   **b.** 20 minutes   **c.** 40 minutes
    d. 45 minutes   **e.** 50 minutes

Q3. A woman walks for 15 miles in 3 hours. At what speed does the woman walk?

    a. 45 mph   **b.** 5 mph   **c.** 20 mph   **d.** 15 mph   **e.** 10 mph

Q4. The distance between campsite A and campsite B is 32 miles. You walk at an average speed of 6 mph. If you set off from campsite A at 0900hrs, what time would you arrive at campsite B?

    a. 1520hrs   **b.** 1410hrs   **c.** 1440hrs   **d.** 1610hrs   **e.** 1420hrs

Q5. A train from Doncaster to Grimsby takes 1 hour 30 minutes. If the train is travelling at 64 mph, what is the distance travelled?

    a. 94 miles   **b.** 96 miles   **c.** 95 miles   **d.** 92 miles   **e.** 98miles

Q6. A yacht sails at 30 mph. You are sailing across the Channel estuary which is 240 miles long. How long does it take you complete your journey?

    a. 8 hours   **b.** 5 hours   **c.** 6 hours   **d.** 4 hours   **e.** 12 hours

Q7. You find a rucksack full of money. In the bag there is a bundle of fifty £10 notes, a bundle of twenty £5 notes and ten money bags of £2 coins, each containing 15 coins. What is the total amount in the rucksack?

    a. 600   **b.** 750   **c.** 825   **d.** 900   **e.** 950

Q8. You annual car insurance costs £240.48. How much is this per month?

    a. £20.04   **b.** £20.02   **c.** £18.04   **d.** £22.02   **e.** £22.06

Q9. During a week of action, the Police carry out four early morning drug raids. On Monday they enter a property at 0710hrs and leave at 0720hrs. On Tuesday they enter at 0810hrs and leave at 0840hrs; on Thursday they enter at 0850hrs and leave at 0905hrs; and on Friday they enter a property at 0700hrs and leave at 0725hrs. What was the average time spent at a property during these raids?

    a. 10 minutes   **b.** 25 minutes   **c.** 20 minutes
    d. 30 minutes   **e.** 45 minutes

Q10. The train to work travels at 70 mph. The distance the train travels is 21 miles. How long does it take to travel to work?

    a. 12 minutes   **b.** 8 minutes   **c.** 18 minutes
    d. 15 minutes   **e.** 16 minutes

Q11. In your money box there are two £5 notes, five £2 coins, three £1 coins, six 10p coins and one penny. How much is in your money box?

    a. £23.61   **b.** £13.61   **c.** £14.61   **d.** £16.41   **e.** £23.41

Q12. A room is 12 metres long and 5 metres wide. A carpet tile is 100cm by 100cm. How many tiles do you need to carpet the entire room?

    a. 30   **b.** 40   **c.** 20   **d.** 6   **e.** 60

Q13. Bread costs £1.25, milk costs £2.13 and a pack of apples cost 66p. How much change will you have from £5?

    a. £0.94   **b.** £0.96   **c.** £1.06   **d.** £1.36   **e.** £1.96

Q14. A TV has been reduced by 20% to £200. What was its original price?

    a. £220   **b.** £240   **c.** £235   **d.** £250   **e.** £300

Q15. In Year 1 you had £200 in savings; by Year 2 this has increased to £230. By what percentage have your savings increased?

    a. 10%   **b.** 12%   **c.** 15%   **d.** 20%   **e.** 25%

Q16. House prices have decreased by 5%. The price of your house before the decrease was £150,000. What is its price now?

    a. £142,500   **b.** £143,000   **c.** £145,000
    d. £146,000   **e.** £147,500

Q17. A car park has 8 floors. When completely full, each floor can hold 230 cars. How many cars in total can fit in the car park?

    a. 1,440   **b.** 1,840   **c.** 2,040   **d.** 2,100   **e.** 2,140

Q18. A sales assistant works 4 days per week. How many days does the sales assistant (without holiday entitlement) work a year?

    a. 182   **b.** 192   **c.** 204   **d.** 206   **e.** 208

Q19. In one year, you arrest 321 people. 119 of these people are charged and the rest are cautioned. How many people are cautioned?

    a. 202   **b.** 198   **c.** 200   **d.** 204   **e.** 206

Q20. John is 6ft 2", Ben is 5ft 9", Sarah is 5ft 4" and Garry is 5ft 7". What is the average height of the group?

    a. 5ft 6"   **b.** 5ft 7.5"   **c.** 5ft 8.5"   **d.** 5ft 9"   **e.** 5ft

Q21. A farmer has 5 identical fields, all of which are square fields. If one side of a field measures 500 metres long, what is the combined total perimeter of all the farmer's fields?

    a. 1,000m   **b.** 10,000m   **c.** 25,000m   **d.** 50,000m   **e.** 100,000m

Q22. In a car park there are 1,200 cars. One sixth of the cars in the car park are blue. How many are blue?

    a. 20   **b.** 100   **c.** 200   **d.** 250   **e.** 400

Q23. In a car park there are 120 cars. Five tenths of the cars in the car park are red. 2/3 of the red cars have five doors. How many red cars have five doors?

    a. 40   **b.** 30   **c.** 20   **d.** 70   **e.** 15

Q24. A toy shop has increased the price of all toy by 15%. If a toy cost £1 before the shop raised all of its prices by 15% how much does this toy cost after a 15% increase?

    a. £1.05   **b.** £1.15   **c.** £1.50   **d.** £2.50   **e.** £3.15

ANSWERS TO PRACTICE TEST 7

ANSWER TO QUESTION 1 (PRACTICE TEST 7)

$$Time = \frac{distance}{speed}$$

$$= \frac{390 \ miles}{90 \ mph}$$

The distance is 240 miles and the speed is 120 miles per hour. Both of these are in the units required to calculate time in hours. Note that because the distance is in miles and speed is in 'miles per hour' when a value for 'time' is calculated this will be time in hours.

$$Time = \frac{240 \ miles}{120 \ mph}$$

$$= 2 \ hours$$

The answer to question 1 (Practice Test 8) is **a.** 2 hours

ANSWER TO QUESTION 2 (PRACTICE TEST 7)

$$Time = \frac{distance}{speed}$$

The distance is 20 miles and the speed is 30 miles per hour. Both of these are in the units required to calculate time in hours. Note that because the distance is in miles and speed is in 'miles per hour' when a value for 'time' is calculated this will be time in hours.

$$Time = \frac{20 \ miles}{30 \ mph}$$

$$= 0.6666666666 \ hours$$

To convert hours into minutes, multiply the hours by 60 as shown below:

$$0.6666666666 \ hours \ in \ minutes = 0.6666666666 \times 60$$

$$= 40 \ minutes$$

The answer to question 2 (Practice Test 7) is **c.** 40 minutes

ANSWER TO QUESTION 3 (PRACTICE TEST 7)

$$Speed = \frac{distance}{time}$$

$$= \frac{15\ miles}{3\ hours}$$

$$= 5\ mph$$

The woman walks at **b.** 5mph

ANSWER TO QUESTION 4 (PRACTICE TEST 7)

$$Time = \frac{distance}{speed}$$

The distance is 32 miles between campsite A and B and the average speed is 6 miles per hour. Both of these are in the units required to calculate time in hours. Note that because the distance is in miles and speed is in 'miles per hour' when a value for 'time' is calculated this will be time in hours.

$$Time = \frac{32\ miles}{6\ mph}$$

$$= 5.3333\ hours$$

5. 3333 hours is the same as 5 hours and 20 minutes. It is important not to confuse '0.333333' hours as being '0.33333' minutes. To convert 0.3333333 hours recurring into minutes, multiply 0.3333333 by 60.

$$0.333333\ hours\ in\ minutes = 0.333333 \times 60 = 20\ minutes$$

This means it took 5 hours and 20 minutes to walk from campsite A to campsite B. If you set off at 09.00 hours, five hours later would make it 14.00 hours. Add another 20 minutes to this would make the time 14.20 hours.

The answer to question 4 (Practice Test 7) is **e.** 1420 hours

ANSWER TO QUESTION 5 (PRACTICE TEST 7)

Distance travelled = Speed × Time taken

The speed is 64 miles per hour and the time taken was 1 hour 30 minutes which is the same as 1.5 hours because 30 minutes is 0.5 of an hour or in other words, half an hour.

Distance travelled = Speed × Time taken

$$= 64 × 1.5$$

$$= 96 \text{ miles}$$

The answer to question 5 (Practice Test 7) is **b.** 96 miles

ANSWER TO QUESTION 6 (PRACTICE TEST 7)

$$Time = \frac{distance}{speed}$$

The distance is 240 miles and the speed is 30 miles per hour. Both of these are in the correct units. Note that because the speed is in 'miles per hour' when a value for 'time' is calculated this will be time in hours.

$$Time = \frac{240 \text{ miles}}{30 \text{ mph}}$$

$$= 8 \text{ hours}$$

The answer to question 6 (Practice Test 7) is **a.** 8 hours

ANSWER TO QUESTION 7 (PRACTICE TEST 7)

50 *ten pound notes* = 50 × £10 = £500

20 *five pound notes* = 20 × £5 = £100

Ten money bags containing 15 *coins each* = 10 × 15 = 150 *coins*

Each coin in the bag is a £2 coin, so 150 × 2 = £300

Total amount in the rucksack = £500 + £100 + £300 = £900

The answer to question 7 (Practice Test 7) is **d.** £900

ANSWER TO QUESTION 8 (PRACTICE TEST 7)

There are 12 months in a year. Therefore, the annual car insurance costs:

$$£240.48 ÷ 12 = £20.04$$

The answer to question 8 (Practice Test 7) is **a.** £20.04

ANSWER TO QUESTION 9 (PRACTICE TEST 7)

On Monday 10 minutes was spent in the property.

On Tuesday 30 minutes was spent at the property

On Thursday 15 minutes was spent at the property

On Friday 25 minutes was spent at the property.

$$Total\ time\ spent\ at\ the\ property = 80\ minutes$$

To calculate the average time, divide the total time spent at the property by the total number of days visited which was 4 days.

$$Average = 80 ÷ 4 = 20\ minutes$$

The answer to question 9 is **c.** 20 minutes

ANSWER TO QUESTION 10 (PRACTICE TEST 7)

$$Time = distance ÷ speed$$

$$= 21\ miles ÷ 70\ mph$$

$$= 0.3\ hours$$

To convert 0.3 hours into minutes, multiply by 60:

$$0.3 × 60 = 18\ minutes$$

The answer to question 12 (Practice Test 7) is **c.** 18 minutes

ANSWER TO QUESTION 11 (PRACTICE TEST 7)

$$Two\ five\ pounds\ notes = 2 × £5 = £10$$

$$Five\ two\ pound\ coins = 5 × £2 = £10$$

Three one pound coins = 3 × £1 = £3

Six ten pence coins = 6 × 10p = 60p

One penny = 1p

Total = £10 + £10 + £3 + 60p + 1p = £23.61

The answer to question 13 is **a.** £23.61

ANSWER TO QUESTION 12 (PRACTICE TEST 7)

Note: the measurement of the room is given in metres and the measurements of a carpet tile are given in centimetres (cm). It is important to be consistent and either use centimetres (cm) or metres (m) throughout your calculations – otherwise you will get a wrong answer.

Using Centimetres

Room (12 metres long and 5 metres wide)

Use the conversion: 1 *metre* = 100 *cm*

12 *metres* in *cm*:

$$12 \ metres = 100 \ cm \times 12 = 1200 \ cm$$

5 *metres* wide in *cm*:

$$5 \ metres = 100 \ cm \times 5 = 500 \ cm$$

Now all the units are in centimetres and the calculations can be carried out.

The area of the room is:

$$1200 \ cm \times 500 \ cm = 600,000 \ cm^2$$

(The units of area are always squared – this is indicated by a small 2 which appears elevated to the top right of the letter 'm'. If you were to tell someone the area of the room in words, you would say: "The area of the room is six hundred thousand centimetres squared")

Area of a carpet tile

A carpet tile is 100 cm wide and 100 cm in length. To calculate the area of the tile, multiply the width by the length:

$$Carpet \ tile \ area = 100 \ cm \times 100 \ cm = 10,000 \ cm^2$$

Now ask yourself how many of these tiles with an area of 10,000 cm2 can fit into a room which has an area of 600,000 cm²?

The easiest way to find out is to divide the two:

$$\frac{Area\ of\ Room}{Area\ of\ a\ tile} = \frac{600{,}000\ cm^2}{10{,}000\ cm^2} = 60$$

60 tiles fit into the room. The answer is **e.** 60

Now try the same question using metres (m) only. Use the conversion $1m = 100cm$.

Your answer should be 60.

ANSWER TO QUESTION 13 (PRACTICE TEST 7)

The easiest way to find how much change you will have left from £5 is to add the individual costs of each item together and then subtract this from £5 as shown below.

Note that 66*p in pounds* = 66*p* ÷ 100 = £0.66

(Divide the pence by 100 to convert into pounds)

$$Bread + Milk + Apples = £1.25 + £2.13 + £0.66 = £4.04$$

In total, the cost of buying bread, milk and apples is £4.04. If you gave a £5 note to pay for these items, you would be given £0.96 (96p) change:

$$£5 - £4.04 = £0.96$$

The answer is **b.** £0.96

ANSWER TO QUESTION 14 (PRACTICE TEST 7)

Call the original price £ *x*. To reduce the original price, £x by 20% follow the steps below:

Step 1: Convert the percentage into a decimal by dividing the percentage by 100.

$$20\% = 20 \div 100 = 0.2$$

Step 2: Subtract the decimal from 1

$$1 - 0.2 = 0.80$$

Step 3: Now multiply the original cost of the house (£x) by 0.80. This will be equal to the price of the TV after a 20% reduction, which is given in the question as £200.

$$£x \times 0.80 = £200$$

Step 4: Rearrange the formula so that it is in terms of £x :

$$£x = £200/0.80 = £250$$

This means that the original price of the TV, before a reduction of 20% was £250. The answer is **d.** £250

ANSWER TO QUESTION 15 (PRACTICE TEST 7)

This question can be solved using the percentage increase formula:

$$\% \ increase = \frac{highest \ value - lowest \ value}{lowest \ value} \times 100\%$$

$$= \frac{£230-£200}{£200} \times 100\%$$

$$= \frac{£30}{£200} \times 100\%$$

$$= 0.15 \times 100\%$$

$$= 15\%$$

The answer is **c.** 15%

ANSWER TO QUESTION 16 (PRACTICE TEST 7)

The price of your house was £150,000 and it has now decreased by 5%. To decrease any number by 5% follow the steps below:

Step 1: Convert the percentage into a decimal by dividing the percentage by 100.

$$5\% = 5 \div 100 = 0.05$$

Step 2: Subtract the decimal from 1

$$1 - 0.05 = 0.95$$

Step 3: Now multiply the original cost of the house (£150,000) by 0.95 in order to find out what the new price is after a 5% reduction.

$$£150,000 \times 0.95 = £142,500$$

This means that the value of the house now after a 5% reduction in price is £142,500

The answer to question 18 (Practice test 7) is **a.** £142,500

ANSWER TO QUESTION 17 (PRACTICE TEST 7)

Each floor can hold 230 cars and there are 8 of these floors. To calculate the total amount of cars that can fit into the car park use the following calculation:

$$230 \times 8 = 1,840 \; cars$$

The answer is **b.** 1,840 cars.

ANSWER TO QUESTION 18 (PRACTICE TEST 7)

There are 52 weeks in a year. If a sales assistant works 4 days a week, then for 1 year the total amount of days they work can be calculated by multiplying 52 by 4.

$$52 \times 4 = 208 \; days$$

The answer is **e.** 208

ANSWER TO QUESTION 19 (PRACTICE TEST 7)

$$Amount \; of \; people \; cautioned = 321 - 119 = 202 \; people$$

The answer is **a.** 202

ANSWER TO QUESTION 20 (PRACTICE TEST 7)

1 *foot* = 12 *inches*

Convert feet into inches by multiplying all the feet by 12 then adding them to the remaining inches.

John's height (6ft 2") in inches = 6 ft × 12 + 2 inches = 74 inches

Ben's height (5ft 9") in inches = 5 ft × 12 + 9 inches = 69 inches

Sarah's height (5ft 4") in inches = 5 ft × 12 + 4 inches = 64 inches

Gary's height (5ft 7") in inches = 5 ft × 12 + 7 inches = 67 inches

To find an average height, add all the heights in inches together and divide by the number of people:

$$Average\ height = \frac{Total\ of\ all\ heights\ added\ together}{Number\ of\ heights\ being\ measured}$$

$$= \frac{74 + 69 + 64 + 67}{4}$$

$$= \frac{274}{4}$$

$$= 68.5\ inches$$

The average height is 68.5 inches. To convert this back into feet divide by 12:

$$\frac{68.5}{12} = 5.70833333...feet$$

Note: 5.70833333 feet DOES NOT equal 5'70833333". In order to calculate what 0.7833333 feet is in inches, multiply by 12:

$$0.7833333 × 12 = 8.5\ inches$$

The average height is therefore 5'8.5" which makes the answer **c.**

ANSWER TO QUESTION 21 (PRACTICE TEST 7)

A square means that all 4 sides are the same length. So if one side of a field measures 500 metres, all the other sides of the field, which are square fields will have the same length.

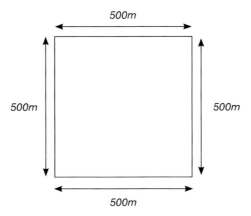

The perimeter of one field can be found by adding together all the 4 sides:

Perimeter of one field = 500m + 500m + 500m + 500m = 2000m

The question asks for the combined total perimeter of all 5 fields. There are two ways of doing this. Method 1 adds 2000 metres together five times and method 2 below multiplies 2000 by 5:

Method 1

Perimeter of all 5 fields combined =

2000*m* + 2000*m* + 2000*m* + 2000*m* + 2000*m* = 10,000 *metres in total*

Method 2

Perimeter of all 5 fields combined = 2000*m* × 5 = 10,000 *metres in total*

The answer is **b.** 10,000 m

ANSWER TO QUESTION 22 (PRACTICE TEST 7)

One sixth, 1/6 of 1,200 cars are blue. Remember that in maths the word 'of' means multiply. To find how many cars are blue the following calculation must be carried out:

Number of blue cars out of the 1,200 cars $= \dfrac{1}{6} \times 1200 = \dfrac{1}{6} \times \cancel{12}(2)00$

$= 200$ *cars*

Note: The 12 from 1200 cancels with the 6 at the bottom of the fraction to leave 2, then the remaining two zeros are attached to the number 2 to give an answer of 200.

If you struggle with fractions try this:

$\dfrac{1}{6} \times 1200$ Is the same as:

$$\dfrac{1}{6} \times \dfrac{1,200}{1}$$

The top half of the fraction and bottom half can now be multiplied separately:

$$1 \times 1,200 = 1,200$$

$$6 \times 1 = 6$$

$$\dfrac{1}{6} \times \dfrac{1,200}{1} = \dfrac{1,200}{6}$$

Finally, work out how many times the number 6 goes into 1,200.

$$\dfrac{1,200}{6} = 1,200 \div 6 = 200$$

The answer is **c.** 200.

ANSWER TO QUESTION 23 (PRACTICE TEST 7)

Five tenths = 5/10 cars are red.

2/3 of these red cars have five doors

To calculate how many of the 120 red cars have five doors, work out what 2/3 of 5/10 equals first. Remember that in mathematics, the word 'of' means multiply. Thus, the calculation to work out what fractions of red cars have five doors becomes:

$$\frac{2}{3} \times \frac{5}{10} = \frac{1\theta}{3\theta} = \frac{1}{3}$$

The zeros from the numerator and denominator of the fraction cancel each other out here.

This means that a third of red cars have five 5 doors.

One third 1/3 can now be multiplied by the total number of red cars given in the question (120) which will give the number of red cars with 5 doors:

$$\frac{1}{3} \times 120 = 40 \text{ } red \text{ } cars \text{ } have \text{ } 5 \text{ } doors$$

The answer is **a.** 40

ANSWER TO QUESTION 24 (PRACTICE TEST 7)

Any number can be increased by a percentage by converting the percentage into a decimal then adding 1 to that decimal and then multiplying the decimal by the number you want to increase by a percentage.

Step 1: Convert the percentage into a decimal by dividing the percentage by 100.

$$15\% = 15 \div 100 = 0.15$$

Step 2: Add 1 to the decimal

$$1 + 0.15 = 1.15$$

Step 3: Now multiply the cost of the toy by 1.15 in order to find out what the new cost of the toy is.

$$£1 \times 1.15 = £1.15$$

This means that the toy has increased in value by 15p and now costs £1.15

The answer to question 26 (Practice test 10) is **b.** £1.15

END OF QUESTIONS AND ANSWERS

CONCLUDING REMARKS

If you are reading this after completing all chapters in this book, well done! I hope that you have picked up techniques which will save you time and effort when solving similar questions in the future whether it be a numerical test for a job you are applying for or simply in everyday life!

Whichever path you may choose to take in life I hope that this book has helped you some way towards your ultimate goals and perhaps your dream job! I wish you all the best for the future.

David Isaacs

STRUGGLING WITH BASIC MATHS?

If you struggled with the maths in this book – such as fractions or algebra do not panic. I recommend a copy of my book – *'GCSE mathematics: How to pass it with high grades'* which will demystify any basic mathematics topic you are struggling with. Available now at WWW.GCSEPRACTICEPAPERS.COM to download as an ebook or as a paperback copy.

WANT TO TRY HARDER QUESTIONS?

I recommend my book *'Advanced Numerical Reasoning'* – available now at WWW.AMAZON.CO.UK as an ebook on amazon kindle or on paperback.